FASHION BEADS

FASHION

BEADS

45 ORIGINAL IDEAS FROM AROUND
THE WORLD FOR MAKING YOUR OWN
DECORATIVE BEADWORK AND
JEWELLERY

SARA WITHERS

THAMES AND HUDSON LTD

First published in Great Britain in 1996 by
Thames and Hudson Ltd, London

British Library
Cataloguing-in-Publication
Data

A catalogue record for this book is
available from the British Library

ISBN 0-500-01697-6

Senior art editor: Clare Baggaley
Designer: Tanya Devonshire-Jones
Photographer: David Sherwin
Photographic assistant: Lee Pattison
Picture researchers: Jo Carlill,
　　　Natalie Rule
Senior editor: Sally MacEachern
House editor: Eileen Cadman
Editor: Sandy Ransford
Backgrounds: Sally Bond
Picture research manager:
　　　Giulia Hetherington
Editorial director: Mark Dartford
Art director: Moira Clinch

Typeset in Great Britain by
　　　Type Technique, London
Manufactured by C H Colour Scan
　　　Sdn. Bhd., Malaysia
Printed by Star Standard Industries
　　　(Pte) Ltd, Singapore

CONTENTS

AMERICA 26

INTRODUCTION

My involvement with beads started in the early 1970s. I organized the stock for a small group of shops that sold imports from India, Afghanistan and Morocco. One of my favourite jobs was sorting the kilos of glass beads that we referred to as "Goulimine" beads. These were the Venetian millefiore beads that were made primarily for the African trade. They were brought back to Europe and the USA by travellers from Morocco.

At that time, when I first saw them, they were being bought from a wholesaler for £15 per kilo. I bought some of those beads for myself, but I didn't really start to think about their history for many years.

Soon, I began supplying glass beads to a few shops around Britain, buying them from a wonderful woman called Zoe Yalland who imported them from India. Then I started designing jewellery with them myself, and realized that I was committed to working with beads!

Two things eventually inspired me to start thinking about the origins and history of beads. The first was Lois Dubin's book *The History of Beads*. This is a wonderfully comprehensive and inspirational record of beads from all over the world. It records their evolution since what is probably the first evidence of them – in a French burial site dating to 38,000 BC. These early beads were made from natural materials such as shell and bone, and were clearly used for personal adornment. The book traces the development of bead making and charts the movement of beads

between different countries and continents since that time.

The second event was a visit to the Arkell Collection at the Pitt Rivers Museum in Oxford.

A. J. Arkell lived and worked in the Anglo-Egyptian Sudan from the 1920s to the early 1950s. He made a collection of beads that illustrates the movement of beads across Africa during that 30-year period. The collection includes documentation giving details of prices, the symbolism of beads, and which ones were popular with which peoples; it also proves early links between India and

Africa through the bead trade. All these details showed the economic and cultural importance of beads. I became fascinated as so many others have done. Beads were no longer just pretty but insignificant items associated with childish or cheap jewellery. As well as being objects of beauty they were important indicators of social and economic history.

In the USA there is a bead museum, currently being moved to Washington DC, which has a comprehensive collection. Bead societies have started thoughout the

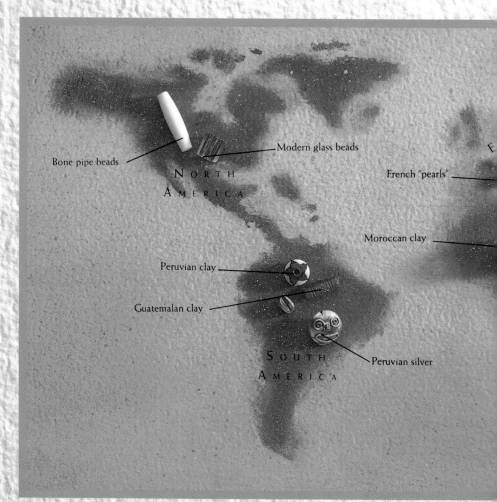

Bone pipe beads

Modern glass beads

NORTH AMERICA

French "pearls"

Moroccan clay

Peruvian clay

Guatemalan clay

SOUTH AMERICA

Peruvian silver

world, bringing together collectors, traders and designers. The wholesale and retail supply of beads has become big business, a far cry from my early days of sending out kilos of beads from my bedroom or office. Thankfully, it has seemed to remain a fairly personal business in keeping with the origins of the trade. Scholars on both sides of the Atlantic are adding to the work started by collectors such as Horace Beck, Van der Sleen, and Arkell. Thus, there are an increasing number of specialized and general books about beads, reflecting this growth of interest.

Our aim in this book is to group the beads from different geographical areas together, and give a little background on their history where possible. We have chosen the designs using two criteria – either the area with which the beads are primarily associated or the ethnic influences for the design of the jewellery. Thus although the Wedding beads on page 124 were made in the former Czechoslovakia, they were intended for the African market, so they are included in the African section. Likewise the rocailles used in the Crow Indian bracelet on page 38 are probably Japanese, but the designer's inspiration is clearly from the Americas. Just occasionally we have had to cross our own boundaries, as in the Eastern influence choker (page 70), but then beads have always moved about!

We have chosen designs that also incorporate a wide range of techniques and styles, our aim being to show both the beads and their potential uses. Most of the beads used in the projects are readily available in Britain and the USA. One or two of the projects are principally inspirational. For example, the polymer clay beads used in Phoenix rising (page 94) were unique creations of the designer. You might be persuaded to try making beads like this yourself. Not all of the instructions dictate exactly what you should do. You can adapt and create variations for yourself, using the particular beads and findings that you have found. As you make your jewellery consider your own personal tastes – for instance, you may want to lengthen or shorten the designs.

There are very few rules when you are working with beads, other than making sure that the threads or wires you are working with are strong enough, and never getting glue onto good beads. Some designers will insist that you should never use nylon monofilament (fishing line) others will use it to great effect. Some use a loom by placing the beads above the warp threads and threading back through from below, others do this in reverse – you must find the ways that work for you. I've mentioned inspiration many times in this introduction. I'd also like to mention enjoyment. I hope that you will achieve both pleasure and satisfaction from making these projects.

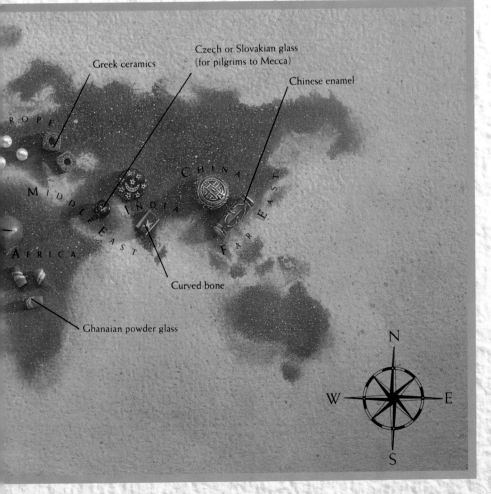

Greek ceramics

Czech or Slovakian glass
(for pilgrims to Mecca)

Chinese enamel

EUROPE

MIDDLE EAST

AFRICA

INDIA

CHINA

FAR EAST

Curved bone

Ghanaian powder glass

N
W   E
S

HOW TO USE THIS BOOK

FASHION BEADS CONTAINS OVER FORTY PROJECTS, MOST OF WHICH CAN BE MADE USING THIS BOOK ALONE. SOME ARE EASIER, OTHERS MORE ADVANCED, AND WE HAVE INDICATED THE DEGREE OF COMPLEXITY IN THE INTRODUCTION TO EACH PROJECT, SO THAT YOU CAN DECIDE WHETHER OR NOT YOU WANT TO MAKE A PARTICULAR DESIGN. SOME OF THE SPREADS ARE INSPIRATIONAL, CONSISTING OF UNIQUE DESIGNS: USE THEM FOR IDEAS, RATHER THAN COPY THEM EXACTLY. ALL THE DESIGNS CAN BE ADAPTED TO YOUR OWN TASTE, OR TO THE ACTUAL BEADS YOU FIND, WHICH MAY DIFFER FROM THE ONES IN THIS BOOK.

Each project has all the information you need. Some are single necklaces or chokers, others are sets of jewellery, with matching earrings or bracelets. You can make one or all of the items according to your own requirements. The projects need different skills to complete them, such as weaving on a loom or using various kinds of wire or findings. The step-by-step text refers you to the relevant section of the Techniques section at the front of the book.

Clear and simple drawings illustrate the techniques needed to complete the projects. They also show how to use the findings listed elsewhere in the book.

Easy-to-follow text supplements the drawings and also provides simple hints and tips about how the techniques may be varied as necessary.

The list of materials provides a complete list of all the beads and findings needed to make each item, as well as the tools and equipment you will need.

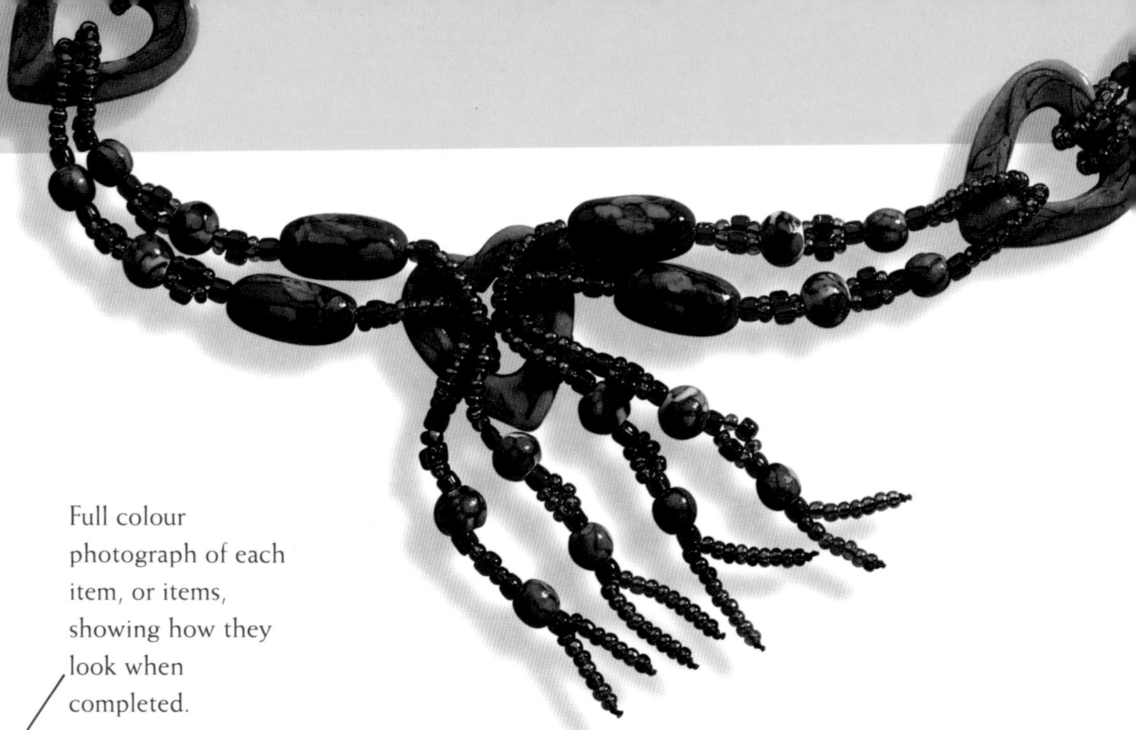

Introductory text gives information about the origins of the beads used in the project and their history.

Full colour photograph of each item, or items, showing how they look when completed.

Leader lines show exactly which part of the item the step-by-step caption is referring to.

Samples of selected beads are shown to help you identify more exactly which beads are used in making each item. You may find beads different to the ones pictured here.

NATIVE AMERICAN INSPIRATIONS 29

1 Cut two 1m (39in) and one 50cm (20in) lengths of thonging. Fold the longer length and attach one spring end. Make a firm knot below it and bring both ends through the first three "bones" and four turquoise beads.

2 Knot the short length of thonging on to these threads and put glue on the knot to secure it. Work another "bone" over the three strands, and another turquoise bead.

3 Separate the strands and thread the pattern, working into the spacer bars.

4 At the large central oval bead, the outside thong runs beside the bead. The middle thong works into the outer hole on the bead and then joins the outside strand. The inside thong goes into a central hole on the oval bead, out at the other side, through a turquoise bead, and back up through the oval bead.

5 This strand now works back up the pendant as the inner thong on the other side, threading through the beads and spacer bars.

6 Start the second side. Knot the inner thong on to the two strands inside the *fourth* "bone".

7 Now work the descending strands in pattern through the beads and spacer bars and through the central oval bead as before.

8 Thread both pairs of thongs into another turquoise bead and another "bone" bead on each side. Then thread all four strands into the last section of beads. Knot at the bottom, using a knitting needle to work the knot close to the beads. Glue the knot, and trim the ends.

FOR THE PENDANT
The basic items listed below and the beads shown opposite:
2.5m (2¾yd) black cotton thonging
2 spring ends
2 x 5mm (¼in) jump rings
1 sprung clasp
4 silver-coloured spacer bars
6 4cm "bone" beads
4 5.5cm "bone beads
8 various silver-coloured beads

45 TURQUOISE BEADS

12 2.5CM "BONE" BEADS

1 SILVER-COLOURED TUBE BEAD

Many European countries have been producers of beads. Italy is perhaps the most well known, with the glass beadmaking techniques that were evident in the Roman trade still being used in Venice today. The Venetian beadmakers attempted to keep their techniques secret, but other countries copied their designs and developed their own specialities, like the deep blue glass Dutch beads. Some of the Venetian secrets were taken to the Czech republic (Bohemia) where a factory was established in 1787.

EUROPE

THE EARLIEST BEADS IN EUROPE WERE MADE FROM SIMILAR MATERIALS TO THOSE USED IN OTHER AREAS, STARTING WITH BONE AND SHELL AND AMBER, AND PROGRESSING INTO THE MANUFACTURE OF FAIENCE AND THEN GLASS BEADS. BALTIC AMBER HAS REMAINED VERY POPULAR THROUGHOUT EUROPE AND THE REST OF THE WORLD. ANOTHER EARLY EUROPEAN SPECIALITY WAS THE USE OF JET FROM WHITBY, WHICH STARTED BEFORE 1400 BC AND REACHED THE PEAK OF ITS POPULARITY IN VICTORIAN BRITAIN.

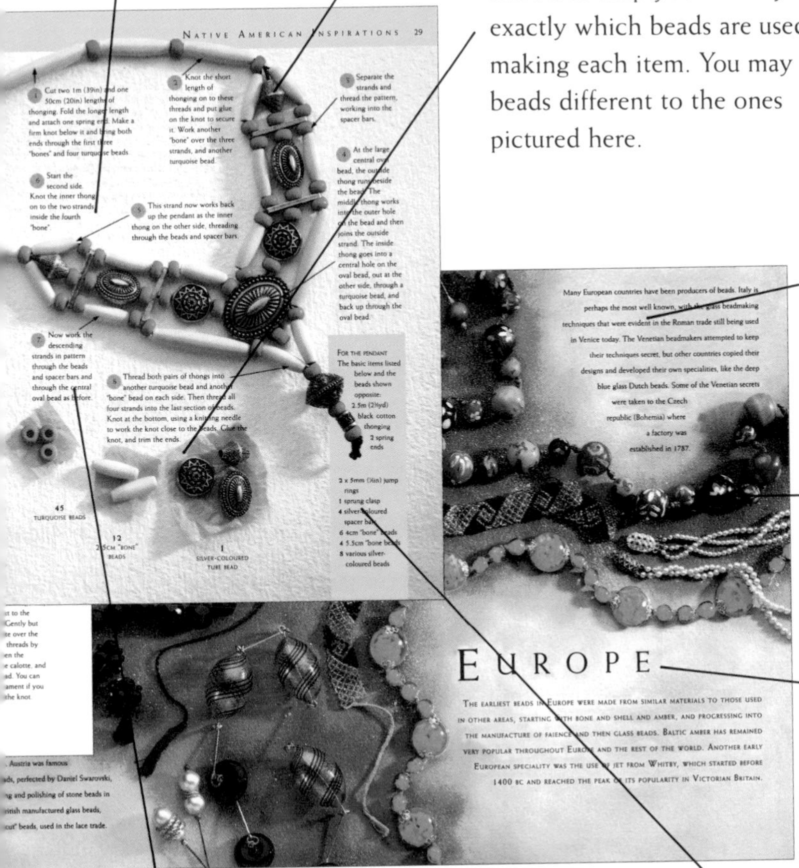

Information is given about the history and types of beads and how they are made and used in each area.

Samples of beads and items of jewellery from each region show the original inspiration for many of the projects. You can find out where to buy these, or similar items, at the end of the book.

The sections are grouped into five geographical areas.

Numbered step-by-step captions give clear and concise instructions for each stage of the project.

If there is more than one item to be made, an additional, separate list of items needed is given.

TOOLS AND EQUIPMENT

MOST OF THE ITEMS LISTED HERE ARE FAMILIAR TOOLS EASILY AVAILABLE FROM CRAFT SHOPS AND HARDWARE SHOPS. KEEP THEM AWAY FROM ANYONE WHO MIGHT WANT THEM FOR PURPOSES OTHER THAN JEWELLERY MAKING!

WIRECUTTERS AND FILES
If you work with wire, a pair of small wirecutters and a light file will be necessary.

TWEEZERS
If you are going to do a lot of beadwork or knotting, fine-pointed tweezers will be helpful since everyone makes mistakes and these will help to unravel them.

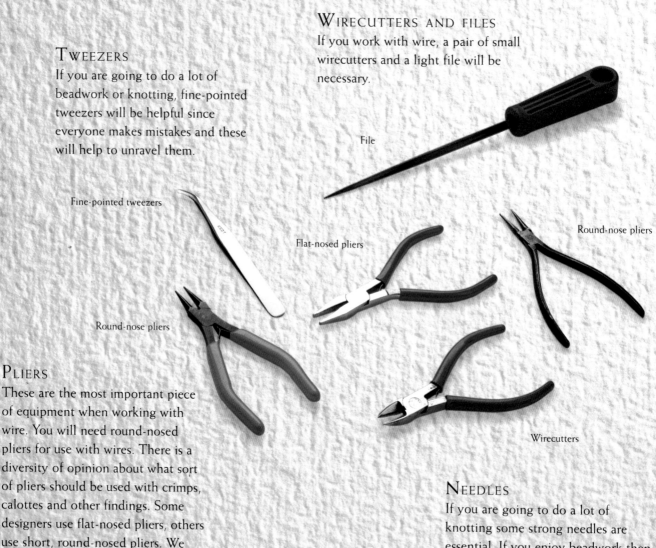

File

Fine-pointed tweezers

Round-nose pliers

Flat-nosed pliers

Round-nose pliers

Wirecutters

PLIERS
These are the most important piece of equipment when working with wire. You will need round-nosed pliers for use with wires. There is a diversity of opinion about what sort of pliers should be used with crimps, calottes and other findings. Some designers use flat-nosed pliers, others use short, round-nosed pliers. We have often referred just to "necklace pliers", so that you can decide for yourself. It is helpful to use pliers with shorter "noses" so that you have close contact with your work.

NEEDLES
If you are going to do a lot of knotting some strong needles are essential. If you enjoy beadwork then you will need fine needles for beadweaving, and some beading needles for use with a loom.

LOOM

It is advisable to use a wooden loom, rather than a metal one which tends to offer a lot of resistance to your work.

Thin polyester thread

THREADS

Designers use different threads, and different beads require different threads. What follows are descriptions of some of the threads available.

NYLON MONOFILAMENT is readily available (as fishing line), inexpensive and easy to thread with. It can be finished with french crimps or by knotting under calottes. Sometimes it shrinks a bit so it is best to leave a small gap before finishing your work.

TIGER TAIL (soft line) is a nylon coated steel wire, available in different gauges. It is strong and easy to thread with, and needs to be finished with french crimps. Be careful when using it as any kinks will weaken it and it can snap where it has been kinked.

POLYESTER THREADS are also very strong and come in a wide range of thicknesses. The very fine ones are excellent for beadwork and can be used with needles. (There are also fine "invisible" threads available for beadwork.) The thicker polyester threads often come in a waxed form to make them more easy to work with. These can be used with french crimps, calottes and knots and are ideal if you want to make a feature of your knotting.

Thick polyester thread

OTHER EQUIPMENT

Some of the more advanced projects in this book require other equipment, and this is detailed beside them, as are the day-to-day objects such as glue and scissors. Finally, the great joy of working with beads is that you can work almost anywhere, but don't forget that you do need good light. There is nothing more frustrating than finding in daylight mistakes you made while working in poor artificial light.

OTHER THREADS can range from silks to linens to leather thonging, again they can be made a feature of your work and used in many different ways. As with all aspects of bead jewellery making think about the beads that you want to use and the effect that you are hoping to create.

FINDINGS

These are all the pieces that hold your work together. A good bead catalogue will have several pages of crimps, calottes, earwires, eye pins, fasteners, spacer bars – the list is long. We have illustrated some of the most common ones to help you to understand the Techniques section and follow the projects in the book. Most findings will be available in a variety of finishes – silver plate, gilt, sterling silver and gold. Your colour preferences are personal, but remember to consider the purity of the metals that you are using, especially on earwires. Nickel is being outlawed by findings manufacturers and suppliers because it causes allergies, so it is important to make sure that you are not using it. Experiment and use different findings as our designers have done. You can often find interesting fasteners on old necklaces. Simple wiring techniques, such as those for making straight earrings (see USING WIRE) usually use ready-made findings like eye pins and head pins. At this point is is also important to mention jewellery wire. As you progress you will enjoy working with jewellery wire which comes in many different gauges and finishes such as brass or silver plated. Again, by experimenting with wires you can extend your range of designs.

We have explained how to use the findings that are in the projects in the Techniques section, but this is a more complete list of the findings that can be used when making bead jewellery

BEAD CAPS ornamental caps to go either side of beads

BELL CAPS for use when finishing multistrand necklaces, to cover the ends (also called END CAPS)

BOLT RINGS secure clasps for fastening necklaces, used with a JUMP RING

BROOCH BACKS glued to interesting beads to make brooches

BROOCH BARS beads can be wired to them to make brooches

CALOTTES squeezed over a knot at the end of a necklace or brooch to attach the fastener, and cover the ends of the thread

CLAMSHELL CALOTTES where the knot is made within the calotte

LACE (or LEATHER) END CRIMPS

CLASPS a large variety of clasps or FASTENERS are available to finish necklaces and bracelets; for example SCREW CLASPS, SPRING BOX CLASPS, TORPEDO CLASPS, TRIGGER CLASPS

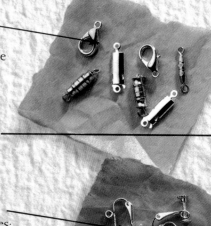

CONES used with multistrand necklaces to cover the ends

EARWIRES used to attach the decorative part of an earring to the ear, available in many different types: EARSTUDS with BUTTERFLY or SCROLL BACKS, FISHHOOK WIRES, HOOPS and KIDNEY WIRES all for pierced ears; EARCLIPS and SCREWS for non-pierced ears (there are also HOOPS that can be hung from earwires)

EYE PINS have ready-made loops at one end and are used to thread the pattern of beads for a straight earring

FRENCH CRIMPS often referred to as CRIMPS – small metal circles that can be squeezed over threads to attach a fastener

SIEVE used with lots of beads to make a brooch, earrings or centrepiece

SPLIT RINGS like a jump ring, but a double circle of wire, safer in use

GIMP very fine wire tubing used for protection over the thread where a fastener is attached

SPACER BARS for multistrand chokers, necklaces or brooches to separate the strands of beads; also used for elaborate earrings

HANGERS come in many different varieties, usually very ornamental, they have a different number of holes in them and are used to finish multistrand necklaces, or to make elaborate drop earrings

HATPINS (also called STICK PINS) long hardened pins with pointed ends, they will need a SAFETY END to go with them

SPRING ENDS also used with leather thonging to attach the fastener

TRIANGULAR BAILS triangular shaped wire usually associated with hanging pendants or earrings (there are also ornamental BAILS).

HEADPINS also for use in making straight drop earrings, these have a flat end to hold on the beads

HOOKS there are many decorative hooks available for use as fasteners
HOOK AND EYE again to be used as a fastener for necklaces

FIGURE 8 small loops of wire used for hanging

JUMP RINGS circles of wire, which can be opened; they can be used for hanging, or at the end of necklaces to fasten with a BOLTRING; they are very versatile

TECHNIQUES

THE PROJECTS IN THIS BOOK ILLUSTRATE THE WORK OF A NUMBER OF DESIGNERS, WHO HAVE DIFFERING WAYS OF WORKING WITH BEADS. THIS SECTION EXPLAINS THE TECHNIQUES USED IN THE DESIGNS. WHEN YOU HAVE MASTERED THEM, YOU WILL BE ABLE TO USE THEM IN DIFFERENT SITUATIONS AND WITH A VARIETY OF MATERIALS TO CREATE YOUR OWN DESIGNS.

FINISHING

There are a number of ways of finishing a necklace or bracelet, and sections of work within more complicated designs.

FRENCH CRIMPS

These can be used with all kinds of threading materials, such as nylon monofilament, tigertail, soft flex, polyester and cotton threads. The crimps are available in different sizes, but most findings suppliers offer the size that is ideal for tigertail and nylon monofilament. You can use the crimps to hold two strands together within a multistrand necklace by just squeezing them firmly on to the threads with pliers. To attach a fastener, put two crimps on the thread, put the thread through the fastener and then back through the crimps. Squeeze the crimps firmly, making a neat loop next to the fastener that allows some movement. Trim the loose end. You can make a loop at the end of a thread in the same way without adding a fastener. Putting a needle into the loop helps.

BELL CAPS AND CONES

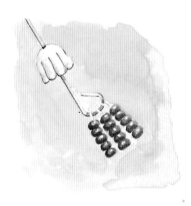

Both of these can be used on multistrand necklaces and bracelets.

Finish the strands with French crimps, making loops as shown above. Join the looped ends either with another looped thread or with a wire, and cover them with a bell cap or cone to hide the ends neatly.

KNOTS

KNOTS USED AT THE ENDS OF A STRAND (as in the Rajasthan necklace, page 86). Before you tighten the knot, insert a needle into it and draw the knot back towards the beads, so the work is held firmly without gaps between the beads. This method, and that described below, can also be used for knotting between beads.

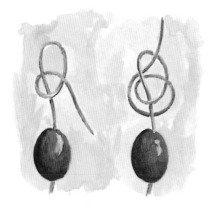

DOUBLE KNOTS are useful for beads with larger holes, or just for extra safety. Wind the thread round your finger twice. Insert a needle in the knot and draw it back towards the beads, as above. Put a drop of clear glue on a final knot (for tassels, etc.), but ensure none goes on the beads, as it will ruin them.

KNOTS TO FINISH

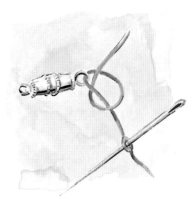

If you want to attach a fastener without other findings, or to make a feature of the knots follow the steps below.

1 Make a simple knot about 5cm (2in) from the end of the thread (further away if you want to make a number of knots). Leave a needle in this knot.

2 Attach the fastener with another knot, allowing space for more knots between the first two.

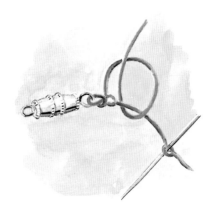

3 Put the thread through the needle and take the needle through the first knot, to secure the thread. You can add a drop of glue to this knot if you think it necessary, but don't let it touch the beads.

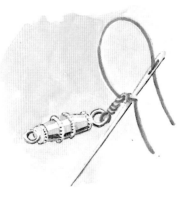

CALOTTES

These can be used to attach fasteners. Knot one end of the thread, or knot two threads together, positioning the knot next to the beads, as shown above. Gently but firmly squeeze the calotte over the knot. Don't damage the threads by squeezing too hard. Open the fastener to hook into the calotte, and trim the end of the thread. You can also knot nylon monofilament if you are using a calotte over the knot.

SPRING ENDS

Spring ends are used mainly with leather or cotton thonging. Place one over the end of the thonging and squeeze the last coil of the spring with pliers. If the leather is very thin, double it over.

LACE END CRIMPS

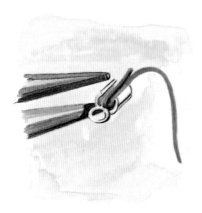

Also called leather end crimps, these are also used with leather or cotton thonging. Put one under the end of the looped thong. With pliers, press one side down over the thong, then the second side over the first.

USING WIRE

These techniques include using eye pins, head pins and jewellery wire. When working with wire it is important to practise the techniques and keep a record of the lengths of wire used in a design, so that you can duplicate them if necessary. Before talking about the potential of wire, there are two things to

mention. First, *fatigue* in your wire: sometimes when you are using an eye pin you will feel with your pliers that the metal is no longer smoothly pliable; always reject these pieces and use another. Secondly, cutting wire: use wire cutters, or pliers with a cutting edge can be very useful. Another way to reduce the length of a piece of wire is by *fatiguing* it: hold it between the points of the pliers and gently move the wire backwards and forwards until it breaks cleanly.

MAKING LOOPS IN EYE PINS OR HEAD PINS.

1 To make straight earrings or hanging pieces within a design, thread the beads on to the pin and allow approximately 8mm (^{3}/$_8$in) of wire above them for the loop (more for larger loops). Bend the wire towards you with pliers to an angle of about 45°.

2 Move the pliers to the top of the wire and roll it away from you, around the pliers. If you do not complete the loop in one movement, take out the pliers, reposition them, and roll the wire again until you have a neat loop at the top.

TO MAKE A FIGURE 8 FINDING make an identical loop going in the other direction above the first one.

OPENING LOOPS

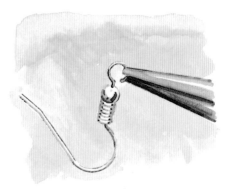

When adding an earwire to your earrings, or when joining two sections together, always open the loops sideways. If you feel the metal has become fatigued, use a new earwire or eye pin.

MAKING JUMP RINGS

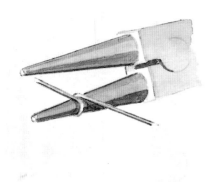

1 If you prefer to make your own jump rings rather than use ready-made findings, wind 0.8mm jewellery wire round your pliers.

2 Neatly clip through the ends of the wire where they make a circle with a pair of wire cutters. To make several jump rings of the same size, wind the wire round a knitting needle or pen to form several circles, then clip through all the rings. Again, open these rings sideways.

MAKING HOOP EARRINGS

1 You can make hoops for earrings in the same way as jump rings if you wind round a larger object. Then clip the wire, allowing an overlap on both sides.

2 Make a loop on one side of the wire with the pliers, thread on the beads, then make another loop on the other side of the hoop.

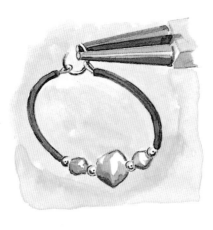

3 Bend up the loops so that they are at right angles to the hoop, and join them with a jump ring.

MAKING HOOKS

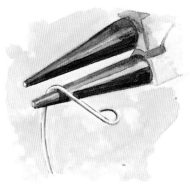

1 Make light hooks with 0.8mm jewellery wire; and stronger ones with 1.2mm wire. Cut a length of wire with wire cutters, depending on the size of hook you want to make. File one end of the wire and make a small loop in it.

2 Bend the wire round the pliers with your fingers into a hook shape.

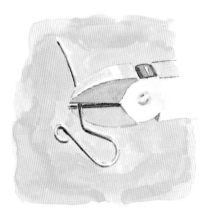

3 Make another little bend in the wire level with the beginning of the first loop, clip off the end of the wire, and file it smooth.

MAKING "EYES"

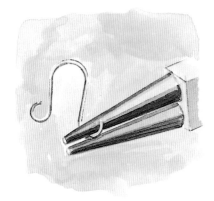

1 Choose the gauge and length of wire according to the strength and size of the "eye" you need. Cut a piece of wire and roll one end. Bend the middle of the wire round the pliers with your fingers.

2 Roll the other side of the wire to match the first.

ORNAMENTAL WIRE COILS

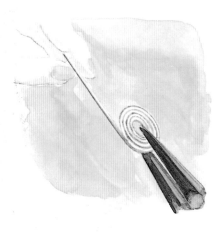

1 Use 0.8mm wire, approximately 6cm (2¹⁄₃in) long, depending on the size you want. Make a loop in one end of the wire, turn the wire on its side and hold it between the pliers. Coil the wire round the loop with your fingers.

2 Leave 8mm (³⁄₈in) at the end to make a loop so you can hang the coil. If the coil is going to be threaded on a necklace, turn the loop at right angles to it.

SECURING LOOPS

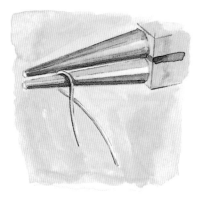

1 This technique secures the beads and is also ornamental. Cut the wire, allowing plenty of length at both ends. Make a loop in one end of the wire, leaving a tail. Hold the loop with the pliers and wrap the tail neatly round the wire below the loop, coiling it several times.

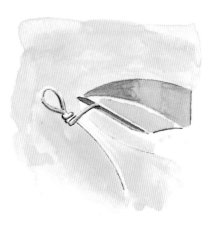

2 Clip off the end of the wire and press the last coil so there are no sharp pieces sticking out. Thread beads on the wire beside this secure loop, then repeat at the other side.

WIRING TO HANG

1 You may have an object you wish to incorporate into a design that doesn't have an appropriate hole, for example, a semi-precious "donut". Cut a piece of wire to go through it, allowing plenty of length. Fold the wire through it leaving one end longer than the other.

2 Roll the shorter end into a loop not too close to the "donut". Coil the longer piece of wire round the bottom of the loop with your fingers. Clip the end, and press it into the coils. In some designs you can wrap your piece several times before you make the loop above it, giving scope to add extra pieces.

BEADWORK

This term relates to the more complicated types of work with beads, such as weaving and loom work. It is usually used for small beads such as rocailles (also called seed beads or pound beads) and bugles (small glass tubes). However, some of the simpler weaving techniques can also be used with larger beads, as in the Thai Silver belt on page 100. The ordinary processes of stringing or wiring beads are not generally referred to as beadwork.

SIMPLE WEAVING

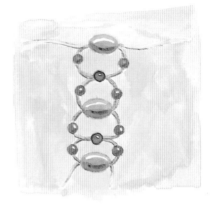

3 Continue in this way until the piece is the length that you require.

1 Work with two lengths of thread, using needles to thread the beads. Put a few beads on each thread, then thread into a vertical bead from both sides, so the threads cross within the bead.

2 Add another bead on each thread and then thread into the next vertical bead, again working from both sides.

WEAVING A BAND

1 To make a band of rocailles (or bugles – the same instructions apply), thread the first row with twice the number of rocailles needed for the width of the band. Bring the needle back through the first half of the rocailles.

3 From the bottom of the second row thread another lot of rocailles, then thread back into the second row. Work back into the third row and add more rocailles to make the fourth, and continue, working back into the previous row each time until the band reaches its required length.

2 Thread on the next rocaille and continue to work between the rows. More rows of rocailles can be added in the same way.

FRINGES AND HANGING BEADS

1 To make a fringe, thread down through the beads you wish to hang and use a bead at the bottom to secure them. Bring the needle back up through the hanging beads, excluding the bottom bead. In this way it will hold the others in place. To add extra detail you can use a little group of beads at the bottom of the fringe.

WEAVING TO BUILD

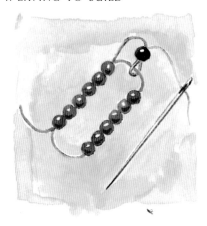

1 To add extra rows of beads to a woven or loomed band, bring your thread through one of the rows of rocailles and thread on a new rocaille. Bring the needle towards you, under the thread that joins the two rows of rocailles, and work back up through the new rocaille.

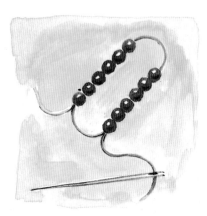

2 Work back down the second half so that you have two rows of rocailles side by side.

LOOMWORK

THREADING A LOOM

1 Cut the warp (lengthways) threads 20-25cm (8-10in) longer than the piece of work. You will need one extra warp thread than the number of rocailles in each row (or three extra if you use the outside warps double – it is often advisable to have two warp threads on the outside rows.) When you have cut the threads, knot them at one end and place the knot under the pin on the roller at the far end of the loom.

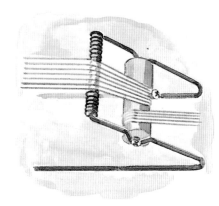

2 Tie the warp threads to the pin at this end and tighten the wing nut, making sure the warp threads are taut before you start work.

2 Hold the rocailles in place with your finger, and bring the needle and thread back through them, above the warp threads. Repeat with the next row and continue in this way, pushing the rows firmly together from time to time. Work the loose ends back into the rocailles when you add new weaving threads. Finish by working the warp threads back into them as well.

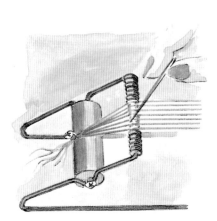

If you are using long warp threads, wind most of the thread on to the roller at this end. Tighten the wing nut and bring the threads towards you, separating them between the spacers with a needle, and placing them into the corresponding spacers at the near end of the loom.

WEAVING ON A LOOM

1 Tie a long piece of thread to an outside warp thread and weave it through the warp threads a few times to give extra strength. Put the rocailles on the needle and pass it beneath the warp threads.

WORKING WITH THREADS

KNOTTING BETWEEN BEADS

Traditionally, knotting was put between beads to protect them from clashing against each other, and to minimize the loss if the threads broke. Modern threads are less likely to break, but knotting can look very attractive and will add to the length of your design. When knotting allow *plenty* of thread – at least twice the length of the proposed finished necklace. The amount of thread needed will depend on the size of the beads and whether you are using double or single knots. You can use both of these (see page 15). There are also methods of knotting that we haven't covered in this book. Use a sturdy needle to position knots correctly, as shown in Finishing.

BUTTONHOLING

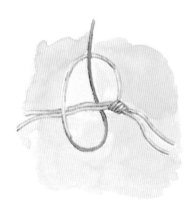

You can use this technique to bind the threads of a multistrand necklace, or use it with other knots to form a fastening loop. Knot a new thread on to the thread that you are working over, make a loop in the thread, bring the end through it and draw it tight. Continue in this way.

HALF KNOTS

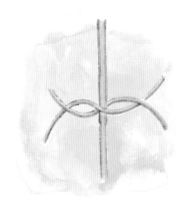

These are also known as macramé braiding, and are ideal for finishing multistrand necklaces, either with the threads holding the beads, or by adding new threads. You need two working threads and one or more core threads. The movements of the working threads are: move the left thread under the core threads and over the right thread; the right thread over the core threads and under the left thread. Continue in this way and the knots will automatically spiral.

OVERHAND KNOT

This simple knot is used above the beads in the Knotwork Pendant on page 98.

SQUARE KNOTS

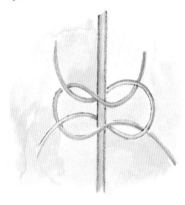

These are similar to half knots but are flat. Again you need two working threads and one or more core threads. Start in the same way, taking the left thread under the core threads and over the right thread; then the right thread over the core thread and under the left thread. Then reverse the movement: put the left thread over the core threads and under the right thread; the right thread under the core threads and over the left thread. Continue alternating these two movements.

LARKSHEAD KNOT

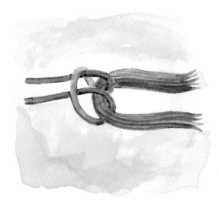

This is ideal for holding bunches of threads together. It is used in the Braided Cord Pendant (page 44), and can also be used when making tassels.

CLOVE HITCHES

These four knots are used in work with areas of knotting, such as the Knotwork Pendant on page 98. All are worked by passing one thread over another.

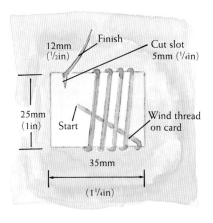

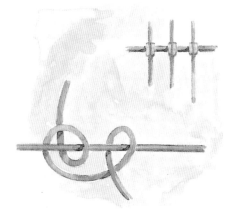

3 Vertical clove hitch, left to right: as above, but vertical.
4 Vertical clove hitch, right to left: as above, but vertical.

2 To hold the threads while braiding: cut 8 pieces of card 25mm x 35mm (1 x 1¼in). Separate the threads into 4 equal groups. Wind each bunch onto the cards as shown.

1 Clove hitch, left to right: the thread loops over first in one direction and then in the other, finishing by passing through the loop.

BRAIDING

This technique is used in the Braided Cord Pendant on page 44. It takes some time to master, but can produce the most rewarding results.

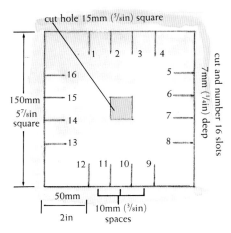

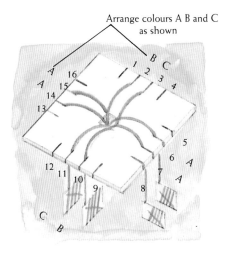

3 Arrange the threads on the board as shown. Refer to the steps below to braid the threads.

Step 1 2->5; 6->9; 10->13; 14->2
Step 2 3->16; 15->12; 11->8; 7->3
Step 3 5->6; 8->7; 9->10; 12->11; 13->14; 16->15

There are specialist books on braiding if you want to explore the subject further.

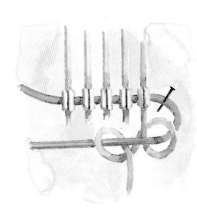

2 Clove hitch, right to left: this is the same as above, but reversed.

1 Cut a piece of card 150mm (5⅞in) square. Cut a hole 15mm (⅝in) square in the middle. Cut four 7mm (¼in) slots along each side as shown and number them.

POLYMER CLAY

MAKING TASSELS

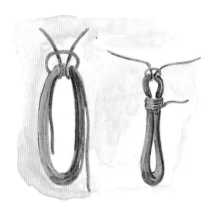

1 Loop a number of lengths of thread together and tie the top with an overhand knot or a larkshead knot.

2 Wind thread round the top of the loops to form the top of the tassel, tucking in the loose ends.

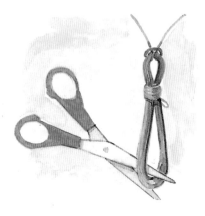

3 Cut across the bottom of the threads to separate them.

TWISTING CORDS

1 This technique is used in the Phoenix Rising necklace on page 94.

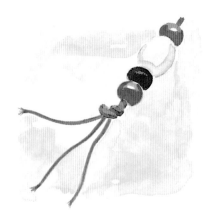

Knot the threads together at the top, then separate them into several bunches.

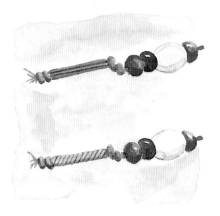

2 Wind each of the bunches clockwise without allowing the rest of the necklace to twist.

3 Knot the threads together again at the bottom and allow the rope you have made to turn back on itself anti-clockwise.

Polymer clays are increasingly being used in modern bead manufacture, not only by polymer clay artists, who are producing beautiful unique designs like the ones shown in Colourful Polymer (page 62) and Phoenix Rising (page 94), but also by mass production methods in countries such as Greece and South Africa. There are several different brands of polymer clays, all of which have slightly different qualities. They can be treated in the same ways, and you will quickly learn how to adjust to their individual properties. All polymer clays are slightly toxic so you should wash your hands carefully after handling them. Always bake them at the recommended temperatures, or slightly below if you are unsure of your oven temperature (your designs won't be harmed by cooking them for a bit longer). When working with polymer clay ensure that you have a clean work surface, and be careful that your colours don't mix (unless you want them to).

PREPARING POLYMER CLAY

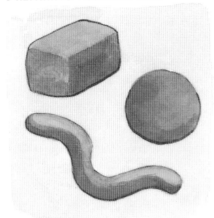

1 The secret of success with polymer clay is to prepare it well before you start work. Start by cutting the block of clay into cubes, usually a quarter of the block that you have bought. Then work it with your fingers, pressing in and out from all sides. Roll it into a ball between your palms, then elongate it into a snake, and bend it back into a ball again. Repeat this sequence until you can work the clay without it cracking or crumbling.

MAKING BEADS

There are many ways to use polymer clay for beadmaking. Colours can be mixed for a marbled effect, or used in stripes, checks, spots – whatever ideas come to you. Another approach is to build up "canes" in the same way that glass makers make canes to pattern millefiore beads. We would suggest that you study a specialist book if you are keen to follow this up. Alternatively, ready-made canes are becoming available, which certainly make bead making easier.

If you want to mix or marble your clay colours, do this first; otherwise start by rolling the clay into a long cylinder. Cut it into equal lengths.

Press in the canes (if using) to pattern the beads. Lightly roll the pieces by hand to shape the beads.

To pierce the beads, hold each one gently between your thumb and forefinger, and work a skewer through, gently rotating it. The beads can be baked on skewers suspended over a baking tray – make sure that they don't touch each other or the oven. Flat designs such as the pendant piece in Phoenix Rising (page 94) can be baked flat on a tray.

AMERICA

IN PRE-COLUMBIAN TIMES THERE WAS A THRIVING TRADE IN BEADS MADE FROM
NATURAL MATERIALS IN ALL PARTS OF THE AMERICAS. WAMPUM, THE TUBULAR
SHELL BEADS SO IMPORTANT IN NATIVE AMERICAN SOCIETY, PERHAPS COME TO
MIND FIRST, BUT SINCE EARLY TIMES BEADS WERE ALSO MADE FROM CLAY,
TURQUOISE, PEARLS, GOLD AND SILVER, AMBER AND JADE. MANY OF THESE
BEADS WERE TAKEN BACK TO EUROPE AFTER 1492, AND AT THE SAME
TIME THE EUROPEAN TRADERS INTRODUCED GLASS BEADS TO
THE AMERICAS.

In South America it is the hand-painted clay beads

from Peru that have become most well known abroad,

but there are many other types of beads being made. There

are clay beads and beautiful dyed soapstone beads from Mexico,

colourful ceramic beads from Guatemala. In Colombia and Peru,

ceramic and stone beads are made using Pre-Columbian designs,

and beautiful amber beads come from the Dominican Republic.

The myth of Manhattan being bought for a handful of beads may have been discounted, but bead trading has always been important in the Americas. As in Africa, the indiginous people were very discriminating about the beads for which they would enter into trade. European traders could encounter severe difficulties if they had the wrong sort. It is the Native American beadwork and work in silver, turquoise and bone, drawing on tribal inspiration, that is considered most synonymous with North America. But American beadmakers are at the vanguard of new designs.

NATIVE AMERICAN INSPIRATIONS

THIS CHOKER AND PENDANT USE MODERN BEADS, BUT THE INSPIRATION COMES FROM THE NATIVE AMERICAN TRIBES OF THE SOUTH-WESTERN UNITED STATES, WHO PRIZED TURQUOISE HIGHLY. THE SILVER-COLOURED BEADS RECREATE THE FEELING OF INTRICATE NAVAHO SILVER WORK; WHILE THE WHITE TUBES REPRESENT PIECES OF BONE, WHICH THE NATIVE AMERICANS USED IN JEWELLERY.

YOU WILL NEED
Necklace pliers
Scissors
Knitting needle or
    similar strong,
    straight object
Glue

FOR THE CHOKER
The basic items listed
    below and the
    beads shown
    opposite:
120cm (4ft) black
    cotton thonging
2 spring ends
2 x 5mm (⅕in) jump
    rings
1 sprung clasp
6 x 3-hole silver-
    coloured spacer
    bars
1 large 5-hole silver-
    coloured oval bead

1 Cut the thonging into three equal lengths and thread the beads as shown, starting with the central five-hole oval bead and working through the spacer bars.

2 At the ends, bring the three strands through the last tube beads and knot them together using a knitting needle to draw the knots close to the beads. Put a drop of glue on the knots to hold them, and trim two of the strands close to each knot.

3 Adjust the length to fit, and attach the spring ends to the remaining strands. Attach the clasp with jump rings.

20
SILVER-COLOURED
TUBE BEADS

18
"BONE" BEADS

1 Cut two 1m (39in) and one 50cm (20in) lengths of thonging. Fold one longer length and attach one spring end. Make a firm knot below it and bring both ends through the first three "bones" and four turquoise beads.

2 Knot the short length of thonging on to these threads and put glue on the knot to secure it. Work another "bone" over the three strands, and another turquoise bead.

3 Separate the strands and thread the pattern, working into the spacer bars.

4 At the large central oval bead, the outside thong runs beside the bead. The middle thong works into the outer hole on the bead and then joins the outside strand. The inside thong goes into a central hole on the oval bead, out at the other side, through a turquoise bead, and back up through the oval bead.

6 Start the second side. Knot the inner thong on to the two strands, inside the fourth "bone".

5 This strand now works back up the pendant as the inner thong on the other side, threading through the beads and spacer bars.

7 Now work the descending strands in pattern through the beads and spacer bars and through the central oval bead as before.

8 Thread both pairs of thongs into another turquoise bead and another "bone" bead on each side. Then thread all four strands into the last section of beads. Knot at the bottom, using a knitting needle to work the knot close to the beads. Glue the knot, and trim the ends.

44
TURQUOISE BEADS

12
2.5CM "BONE" BEADS

8
VARIOUS SILVER-COLOURED BEADS

FOR THE PENDANT
The basic items listed below and the beads shown opposite:
2.5m (2 2/3yd) black cotton thonging
2 spring ends

2 5mm jump rings
1 sprung clasp
4 spacer bars
6 4cm "bone" beads
4 5.5cm "bone" beads
1 5-hole silver bead
2 smaller 1-hole silver oval beads
2 round silver beads
2 "triangular" beads
1 ornate silver bead

PRE-COLUMBIAN INSPIRATIONS

THESE TWO BEAUTIFUL NECKLACES USE PERUVIAN AND GUATEMALAN BEADS IN LOVELY SOFT COLOURS, COMPLEMENTED BY SILVER BEADS FROM PERU. THE FIRST NECKLACE HAS A MIXTURE OF CERAMIC BEADS FROM BOTH COUNTRIES AND PERUVIAN SILVER BEADS AND FEATURES TINY PERUVIAN FIGURES KNOWN AS *IDOLOS* REPRESENTING FERTILITY SYMBOLS, AT ITS ENDS. THE SECOND NECKLACE USES HAND-CARVED MACHU PICCHU STONE BEADS, ALSO FROM PERU, WHICH ARE MADE TO PRE-COLUMBIAN DESIGNS THAT HAVE NOT BEEN USED FOR OVER 500 YEARS. THEY ARE COMPLEMENTED BY PERUVIAN SILVER BEADS INSPIRED BY INCA DESIGNS.

YOU WILL NEED

Round-nosed pliers with very fine points
Necklace pliers
Wire cutters

FOR THE FIRST NECKLACE

The basic items listed below and the beads shown opposite:

2 7mm (¼in) jump rings
6 3mm (⅛in) jump rings
1 5mm (⅛in) jump ring
1 silver hook
20 gauge silver wire
6 silver bead caps
4 silver and brass sun shapes
2 tiny silver *idolos*
9 granulated silver discs
8 Peruvian oval glazed beads
3 Peruvian melon-shaped glazed beads
4 silver beads in two different designs
3 silver round beads

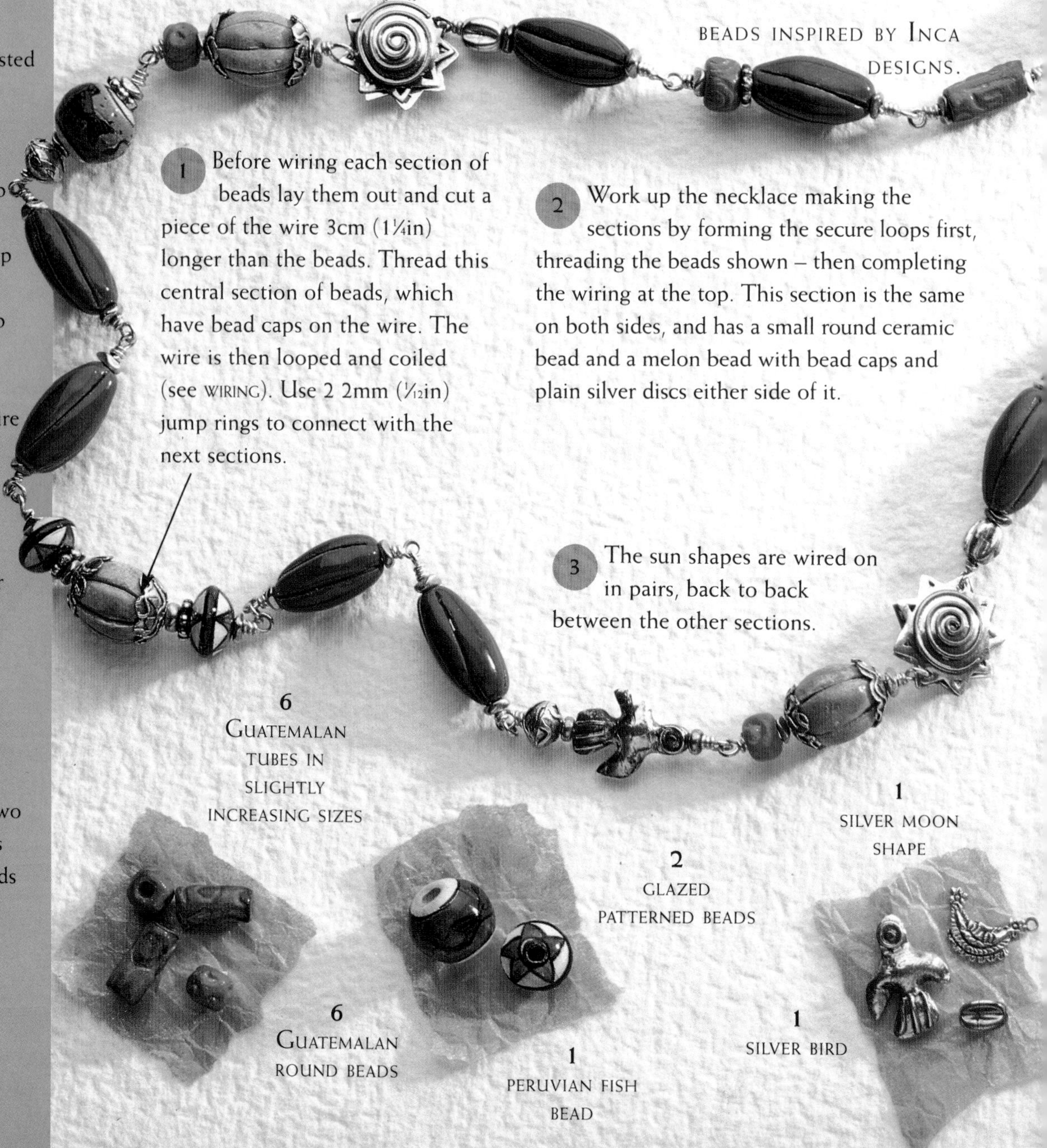

1 Before wiring each section of beads lay them out and cut a piece of the wire 3cm (1¼in) longer than the beads. Thread this central section of beads, which have bead caps on the wire. The wire is then looped and coiled (see WIRING). Use 2 2mm (¹⁄₁₂in) jump rings to connect with the next sections.

2 Work up the necklace making the sections by forming the secure loops first, threading the beads shown – then completing the wiring at the top. This section is the same on both sides, and has a small round ceramic bead and a melon bead with bead caps and plain silver discs either side of it.

3 The sun shapes are wired on in pairs, back to back between the other sections.

6
GUATEMALAN TUBES IN SLIGHTLY INCREASING SIZES

6
GUATEMALAN ROUND BEADS

1
PERUVIAN FISH BEAD

2
GLAZED PATTERNED BEADS

1
SILVER BIRD

1
SILVER MOON SHAPE

5 Here there is a 2mm (¹⁄₁₂in) jump ring below the *idolos*, a 5mm (¹⁄₅in) oval jump ring above it, with the moon hanging on another 2mm (¹⁄₁₂in) jump ring. Finally there is a 7mm (¼in) jump ring and the silver hook.

4 Finish with a tiny *idolos* between two 2mm jump rings and a 7mm (¼in) jump ring at the end.

1 Cut a piece of wire, make a tiny loop at the bottom of it, put this through one of the silver faces, then roll the top of the wire.

3 Thread the beads onto a 70cm (28in) tiger tail, then crimp onto the jump rings at each end and finish with the silver hook.

2 Wire round the donut (see USING WIRE), wrapping round it several times, and picking up the loop at the top of the face bead at the same time.

5
BRASS DISCS

37
PLAIN SILVER
DISCS

16
PERUVIAN OVAL
CERAMIC BEADS

3
SILVER FACE BEADS

2
LONG OVAL
MACHU PICCHU
STONE BEADS

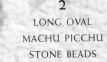

FOR THE SECOND NECKLACE

The basic items listed below and the beads shown opposite:

1 Machu Picchu stone "donut"
4 patterned ceramic beads
6 plain round ceramic beads
2 triangular Machu Picchu stone beads
2 square Machu Picchu stone beads
1 round Machu Picchu stone bead

1 long flat Machu Picchu stone bead
10 brass discs
33 plain silver discs
2 granulated silver discs
2 round silver balls
2 7mm (¼in) jump rings
1 silver hook
4 French crimps
Tiger tail
Jewellery wire
4 silver bead caps
3 silver round beads in two different designs

JABONCILLO AND CERAMICS

THIS IS ANOTHER WONDERFUL MIXTURE OF SOUTH AMERICAN BEADS, WITH JUST A FEW TINY MOROCCAN TILE BEADS WORKED IN FOR GOOD MEASURE. THE LOVELY SOFT, SHINY JABONCILLO (SOAPSTONE) BEADS, THE ROUND CERAMIC BEADS AND THE CRAZY CERAMIC FISH ARE FROM MEXICO. THE SQUARE CERAMIC BEADS AND THE EXQUISITE LITTLE CLAY BIRDS ARE MADE IN COLOMBIA.

YOU WILL NEED
Round-nosed pliers
Scissors
Strong needle
Glue

FOR THE NECKLACE
The basic items listed
  below and the
  beads shown
  opposite:
7.5m (8¼yd) natural
  waxed thread
4 50mm (2in) eye
  pins
4 fish with holes
  across body
9 round ceramic
  beads
34 square ceramic
  discs
20 small round
  ceramic discs

1 Put an eye pin through each of the fish with the hole running through their bodies, and roll the ends, so the loops at each end match.

2 Cut four 1m (39in) lengths of thread and work on the beads in little groups, knotting between the groups, (see FINISHING).

3 Thread tile beads along the fish on eye pins between the loops.

5 Add a 1.5m (5ft) length of thread, folded in half, to each side for the braiding. You can put a spot of glue where you attach the thread to stop it slipping.

4 When your strings look well balanced, bring all the threads through a round ceramic bead at each end.

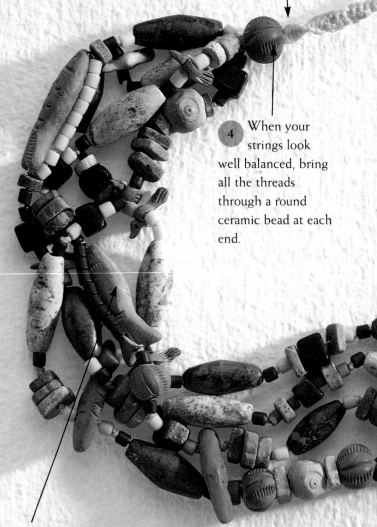

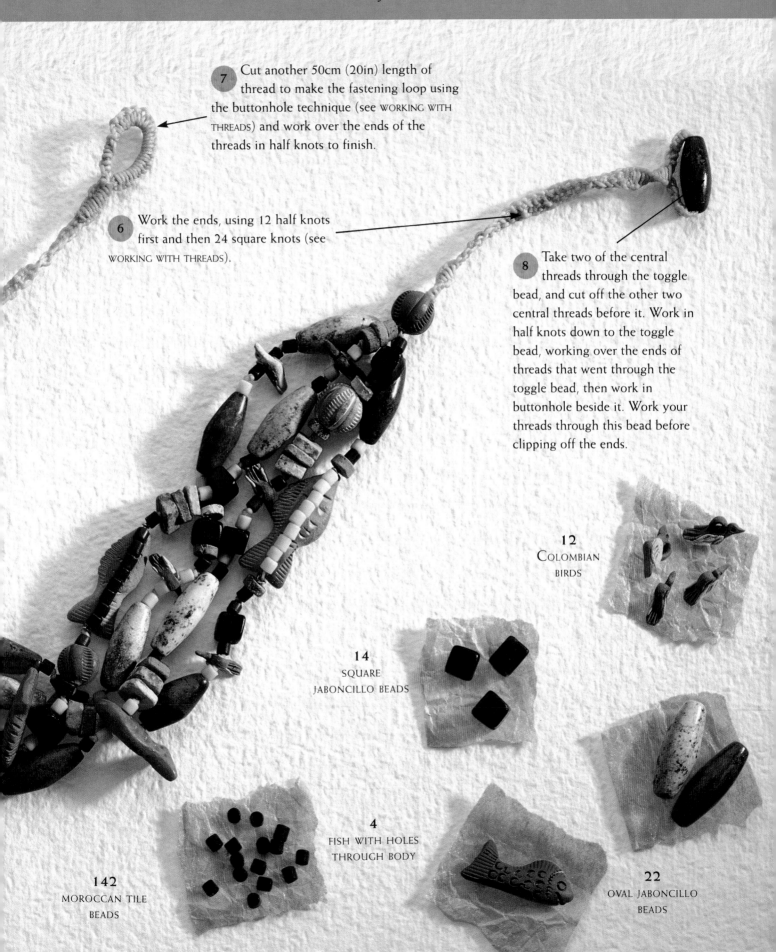

7 Cut another 50cm (20in) length of thread to make the fastening loop using the buttonhole technique (see WORKING WITH THREADS) and work over the ends of the threads in half knots to finish.

6 Work the ends, using 12 half knots first and then 24 square knots (see WORKING WITH THREADS).

8 Take two of the central threads through the toggle bead, and cut off the other two central threads before it. Work in half knots down to the toggle bead, working over the ends of threads that went through the toggle bead, then work in buttonhole beside it. Work your threads through this bead before clipping off the ends.

12
COLOMBIAN
BIRDS

14
SQUARE
JABONCILLO BEADS

4
FISH WITH HOLES
THROUGH BODY

22
OVAL JABONCILLO
BEADS

142
MOROCCAN TILE
BEADS

SILVER FEATHERS SET

THIS PRETTY AND DELICATE NECKLACE WITH MATCHING EARRINGS IS MADE FROM TINY "LIQUID SILVER"
TUBES, TURQUOISE HEISHI TUBES, ROUND "TURQUOISE" BEADS, SILVER BALLS AND LITTLE SILVER FEATHERS.
EACH INDIVIDUAL STRAND IS LIGHT AND DELICATE, BUT THE OVERALL EFFECT IS STRONG, ESPECIALLY
WHEN THE NECKLACE IS WORN WITH THE EARRINGS.

1 Start by hanging the feathers from the eye pins, three singly and two double. Add some beads above them: silver-plated balls, "turquoise" beads and turquoise heishi tubes. We have used a tiny silver-plated spring on one as well. Clip the eye pins to the required length and roll the tops.

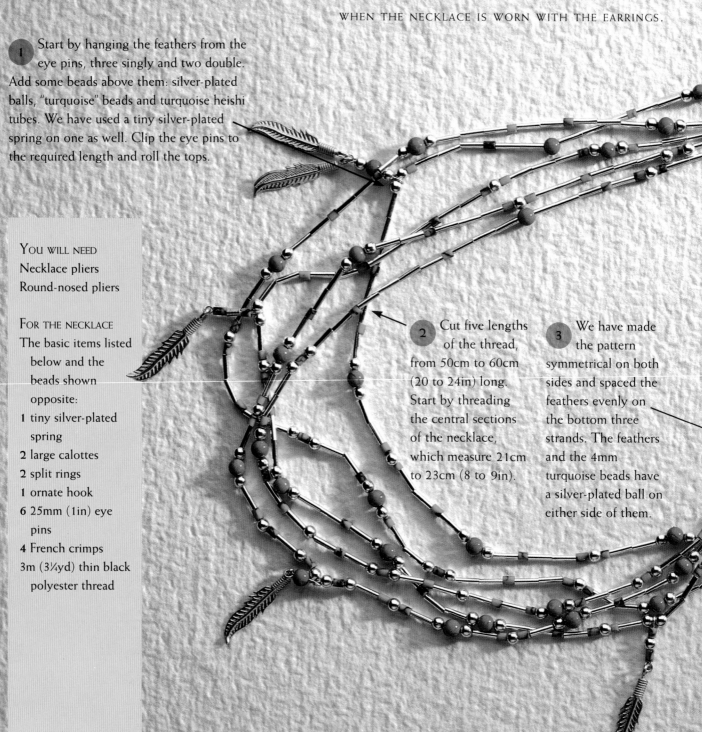

YOU WILL NEED
Necklace pliers
Round-nosed pliers

FOR THE NECKLACE
The basic items listed below and the beads shown opposite:
1 tiny silver-plated spring
2 large calottes
2 split rings
1 ornate hook
6 25mm (1in) eye pins
4 French crimps
3m (3¼yd) thin black polyester thread

2 Cut five lengths of the thread, from 50cm to 60cm (20 to 24in) long. Start by threading the central sections of the necklace, which measure 21cm to 23cm (8 to 9in).

3 We have made the pattern symmetrical on both sides and spaced the feathers evenly on the bottom three strands. The feathers and the 4mm turquoise beads have a silver-plated ball on either side of them.

5 Put a split ring on each calotte, and a hook on one split ring. Squeeze the sides of the hook together to keep it on the split ring.

4 When you are happy with your threading, crimp all the strands together at the ends (see FINISHING), making sure that the crimps won't slip, and squeeze a large calotte over the crimps. Be sure that it is tight, but won't damage the threads.

EARRINGS

1 To make an earring, arrange beads, balls and heishi in your own pattern on four 25mm (1in) eye pins and roll the ends. Join all four eye pins and a silver feather with a jump ring. Put an ear wire into one of the pieces, so that the others hang from it.

2 Make the second earring in the same way, but reverse the position of the hanging pieces.

32
4MM HOWLITE
DYED
"TURQUOISE"
BEADS

270
SILVER-PLATED
TUBES

110
TINY TURQUOISE
HEISHI TUBES

99
3MM SILVER-
PLATED BALLS

7
SILVER FEATHERS

FOR THE EARRINGS
2 silver feathers
16 silver-plated balls
8 25mm (1in) eye pins
2 jump rings
2 silver-plated ear wires
8 4mm howlite dyed "turquoise" beads
4 turquoise heishi tubes

SOUTH AMERICAN DREAMS

THIS FOUR-STRAND NECKLACE USES A MULTITUDE OF DIFFERENT BEADS AND SMALL TREASURES, WHICH ARE WORKED INTO CONES. CHOOSE LITTLE INCA FIGURES, MOTHER-OF-PEARL BIRDS AND PAINTED PERUVIAN BEADS, AND LET YOUR IMAGINATION RUN RIOT.

1 Hang the small sun faces on to the figure 8 findings so that they are ready to thread with the other beads and pendants.

YOU WILL NEED
Necklace pliers
Scissors

FOR THE NECKLACE
The basic items listed below and the beads shown opposite:
1 ceramic sun face
3 small brass sun faces
1 tiny Inca pendant
180cm (2yd) thick black thread
30cm (12in) tiger tail
2 cones
Fastener
14 crimps
3 figure 8 findings
8 Green striped Peruvian beads
116 5mm black glass beads
200 Black rocailles, size 0/7

2 Cut four 45cm (18in) lengths of thread for your main strands and lay them out on your work-surface. The choice and positioning of the beads is up to you, as you will probably have slightly different beads from those we have used.

3 Spread out the more interesting beads and use plainer ones as you reach the ends of the threads. Make the sides of each thread symmetrical. Save enough beads to go on the single strands after the cones, and put four or five of the black rocailles at each end of every thread so they will fit inside the cones.

12
AMBER GLASS
FACETED BEADS

44
BLUE GLASS
FACETED BEADS

12
MOTHER-OF-PEARL
BIRDS

5 When you feel that they are right, make a small loop with a crimp at each end of each thread, leaving the thread tight enough for there to be no gaps, but not so tight that the work becomes rigid. Trim the loose ends of the threads.

6 Cut two 15cm (6in) lengths of tiger tail and make a little loop with a crimp at one end of each piece. Put the small pieces of tiger tail through the loops at the ends of the four strands and then thread the tiger tail back into its own loop, so on each side it is holding all the strands of the necklace.

7 Put a cone on each side and divide the beads that you have left, keeping back two rocailles for finishing. Crimp onto your fastener (see FINISHING) and trim the tiger tail.

22
ORANGE AND
BLUE STRIPED
BEADS

4 The threads need to be slightly different lengths, and those with the heavier pieces should be slightly shorter so the strands will hang together. When you are ready to finish the strands hold them up together in front of you to check how they hang.

10
ORANGE
PERUVIAN BEADS,
ROUND AND
TUBULAR

4
BLUE PATTERNED
PERUVIAN BEADS

4
BLUE STRIPED
PERUVIAN BEADS

2
BROWN
PATTERNED
PERUVIAN BEADS

70
CHIPS HOWLITE
DYED TURQUOISE

CROW INDIAN BRACELET

THE COLOURS OF THIS BRACELET WERE TRADITIONALLY USED BY THE CROW INDIANS FROM MONTANA, USA, WHO WOVE BEADWORK STRIPS WITH WHICH TO DECORATE THEIR CLOTHING ON SPECIAL LOOMS CALLED BOW-LOOMS. THESE WERE MADE FROM BOWS, AND HAD TWO PERFORATED PIECES OF WOOD OR BONE ATTACHED TO THE ENDS TO MAKE SPREADERS TO HOLD THE WARP THREADS. THE INDIANS HELD THE BOW-LOOMS BETWEEN THEIR KNEES WHILE WEAVING THIS BRACELET IS ALSO MADE ON A LOOM.

10 Join a thread to this end and add the fringes here in the same way as on the other side, working back through the rows.

YOU WILL NEED
Bead loom
Beading needles
Graph paper
Scissors

FOR THE BRACELET
The basic items listed below and the beads shown opposite:
Very fine gold wire
2-ply red beading thread
3 Pheasant feathers
4 oval jaspar beads

11 Work the loose threads on this side back into the work. On two of them thread a few rocailles, a 4mm jasper bead and a little loop of rocailles to go round the fastener beads on the other side.

1 Start by drawing the design on graph paper.

4 Work for 30 rows following the design you have drawn. Before making the first piece of fringe, wrap some wire round the ends of the feathers and make little loops for hanging them. Add a citrine chip to each feather as you wire it.

2 Thread your loom (see LOOM WORK). This bracelet has thirty warp threads. Start by threading on 22 beads and work them with a beading needle (see LOOM WORK), increasing by one rocaille on this side after three rows.

3 Increase by one rocaille on each row on this side until you have 28 rocailles.

9 Take your work off the loom and knot the threads into the work. Weave the thread back into the work. Leave two warp threads and add two small lengths of rocailles and 6mm jasper beads to make the fastener in the same way as the fringes.

8 Now decrease to match your rows at the beginning of the bracelet. At the end of the beading, bring your needle back through the rows, adding the fringes of rocailles and 4mm jasper beads in the same way as you added the central fringes.

7 Continue until the pattern is complete. When you reach the final row, add the 4mm jasper beads in the same way as you made the fringe.

6 On the central row of the bracelet, which has the fifth row of fringing, use a 4mm jasper bead instead of a rocaille in the centre of the loom.

11
6MM JASPER
BEADS

15
CITRINE CHIPS

1
LEOPARD JASPER
STONE CHIP

5 Make the fringe by bringing the beading thread out from the loom and adding extra rocailles and jasper beads to it. Secure the fringe either by adding a rocaille to the end, or the loop of a feather. Once this is in place, thread back up the beads and rocailles on the fringe and continue into the next row on the loom.

31
4MM JASPER
BEADS

1
25G (1OZ)
PACKET EACH OF:
RED, BLUE, WHITE
AND MUSTARD
ROCAILLES SIZE
0/10

BAMBOO BIRD'S WING

THE SHAPE AND GRADUATION OF COLOURS IN THIS BEAUTIFUL NECKLACE ARE INSPIRED BY THE PATTERN OF A BIRD'S WING. THE TECHNIQUES USED ARE EMPLOYED BY NATIVE AMERICAN AND MEXICAN BEAD WORKERS; THE CHOICE OF COLOURS AND THE INCLUSION OF BAMBOO STICKS ARE STRONGLY INFLUENCED BY SOUTH AMERICAN INDIAN WORK. ALTHOUGH IT IS AN ADVANCED PIECE, THE BASIC TECHNIQUES ARE RELATIVELY SIMPLE. USE THE INSTRUCTIONS AS GUIDELINES FOR YOUR OWN DESIGN AND COLOURS.

YOU WILL NEED
Scissors
Beading needles
Candle
Varnish

FOR THE NECKLACE
The basic items listed
   below and the
   beads shown
   overleaf:
Transparent nylon
   thread
Black 2-ply nylon
   thread
Very fine brass wire
Cowrie shell
2.5cm (1in) and
   3.5cm (1¼in)
   bamboo sticks
2 25g (1oz) packets
   short rust bugle
   beads
Large semi-precious
   beads

FOR THE CLASP
16 rocailles
3 5mm glass beads
1 semi-precious bead
1 semi-precious chip

2 To start the necklace take a 2m (6½ft) length of nylon thread. Leaving 20cm (8in) at the end, thread on two bugle beads. Bring your needle back through the first, so the two bugles sit next to each other. Pull threads tight. Work thread back down the second bugle. Add a third (See BEADWORK weaving a band). Continue until you have 167 bugles threaded. Go back through each one to reinforce them. You will need to add new threads. Tuck the loose ends into the fringes later.

1 First work on the bamboo sticks. They may be gently turned in a candle flame to darken them. Varnish to stop them smudging.

3 Turn the work so that the thread is on the left. Pick up a rocaille, bring the needle towards you, between the first two bugles. Thread back into the rocaille. Pull the thread tight. (See BEADWORK). Add four more rocailles. Turn, and thread into the bridge between the first two rocailles to create a row of four rocailles. Continue until you have a triangle with one rocaille at the top. Thread back down the side of the triangle.

4 Add two rows of rocailles above the next four bugles. Work another triangle with five rocailles. Work along the top, varying the size of the triangles.

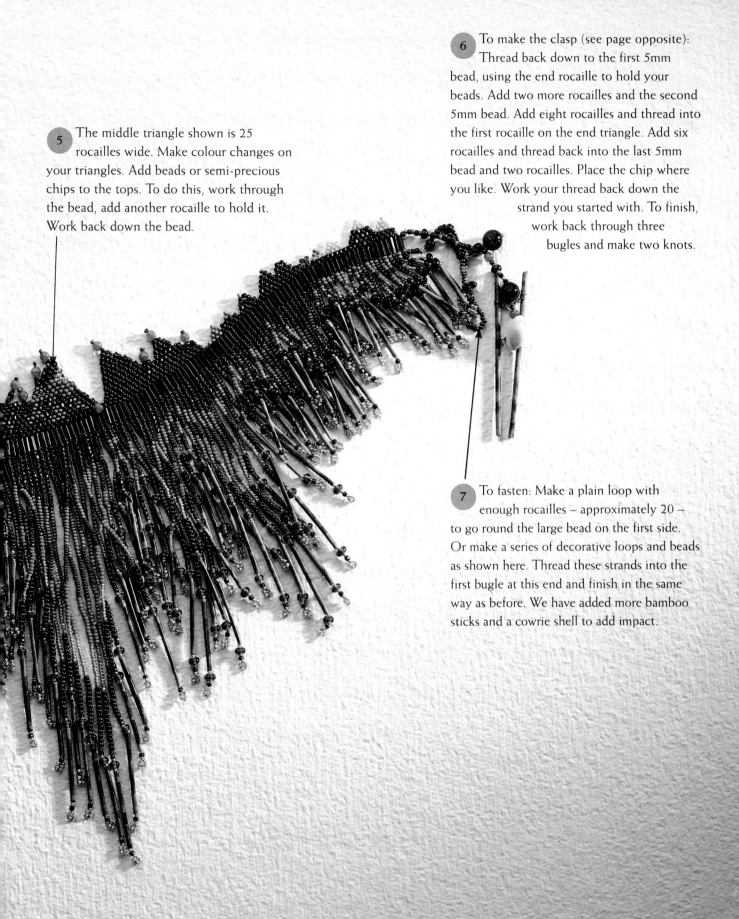

5 The middle triangle shown is 25 rocailles wide. Make colour changes on your triangles. Add beads or semi-precious chips to the tops. To do this, work through the bead, add another rocaille to hold it. Work back down the bead.

6 To make the clasp (see page opposite): Thread back down to the first 5mm bead, using the end rocaille to hold your beads. Add two more rocailles and the second 5mm bead. Add eight rocailles and thread into the first rocaille on the end triangle. Add six rocailles and thread back into the last 5mm bead and two rocailles. Place the chip where you like. Work your thread back down the strand you started with. To finish, work back through three bugles and make two knots.

7 To fasten: Make a plain loop with enough rocailles – approximately 20 – to go round the large bead on the first side. Or make a series of decorative loops and beads as shown here. Thread these strands into the first bugle at this end and finish in the same way as before. We have added more bamboo sticks and a cowrie shell to add impact.

8 For the fringing change to the black 2-ply nylon thread. Work through the bugle. Add ten rocailles, a 5mm bead, another rocaille and a 2.5cm (1in) bamboo stick. Add two rocailles and then another five to make a loop at the bottom. Thread back up into the two rocailles below the bamboo, through the bamboo and the other bead and rocailles. Work up through the bugle and back down the next one to make the next piece of fringe as before.

5MM SEMI-
PRECIOUS BEADS
AND CHIPS

2
25G (1OZ)
PACKETS 5MM
PURPLE GLASS
BEADS

9 Work along the fringe, adding beads to lengthen the pieces and then decreasing again, to create the sort of colour and length changes shown here. Use the smaller bamboo sticks on the outside and the longer ones in the centre. The central and longest piece of fringing has 100 rocailles, a 3.5cm (1¼in) bamboo and a 5mm glass bead.

3
25G (1OZ)
PACKETS EACH
OF: LILAC, DARK
GREEN, GRASS
GREEN, LIME
GREEN ROCAILLES,
SIZE 0/11

3
25G (1OZ)
PACKETS EACH
OF: PURPLE, DARK
BLUE ROCAILLES,
SIZE 0/10

BRAIDED CORD PENDANT

THIS SIMPLE DESIGN ACHIEVES ITS EFFECT WITH A STUNNING GLASS CENTREPIECE AND BRIGHT MODERN AMERICAN GLASS BEADS, STRUNG ON A CORD OF BRAIDED SILKS IN VIBRANT COLOURS THAT HIGHLIGHT THE BEADS. YOU WILL NEED TO WORK CLOSELY WITH THE TECHNIQUES SECTION TO MAKE THIS WONDERFUL CORD.

YOU WILL NEED
Scissors
Needle
1 100g (4oz) fishing
    weight (optional)

FOR THE NECKLACE
The basic items listed
    below and the
    beads shown
    opposite:
310mm (12in) strong
    thin cotton thread
130mm (5in) square
    mounting board
8 25 x 35mm (1 x
    1⅓in) cardboard
    bobbins
1 centrepiece
Silk threads in three
    main colours (half
    in colour A; one
    quarter each in
    colours B and C)
Silk threads to match
    the beads to wrap
    beneath them

1 First work out how much thread you will need. Count how many threads it takes to fill one of the beads until they fit very tightly: you will need 1.5m (60in) of each of these threads. The braid shown here uses 42 green threads (A), 21 blue threads (B) and 21 turquoise threads (C). These are the warp threads.

2 Next prepare your board (see WORKING WITH THREADS) and bobbins, which should have a 5mm (1⅛in) slot in them.

3 Fold the warp threads in half and use the cotton to form a larkshead knot (see WORKING WITH THREADS) to secure them at midpoint. Tie off the warp threads, allowing 8cm (3¼in) for a tassel (see WORKING WITH THREADS).

10
GLASS BEADS IN
VARYING SIZES
AND COLOURS

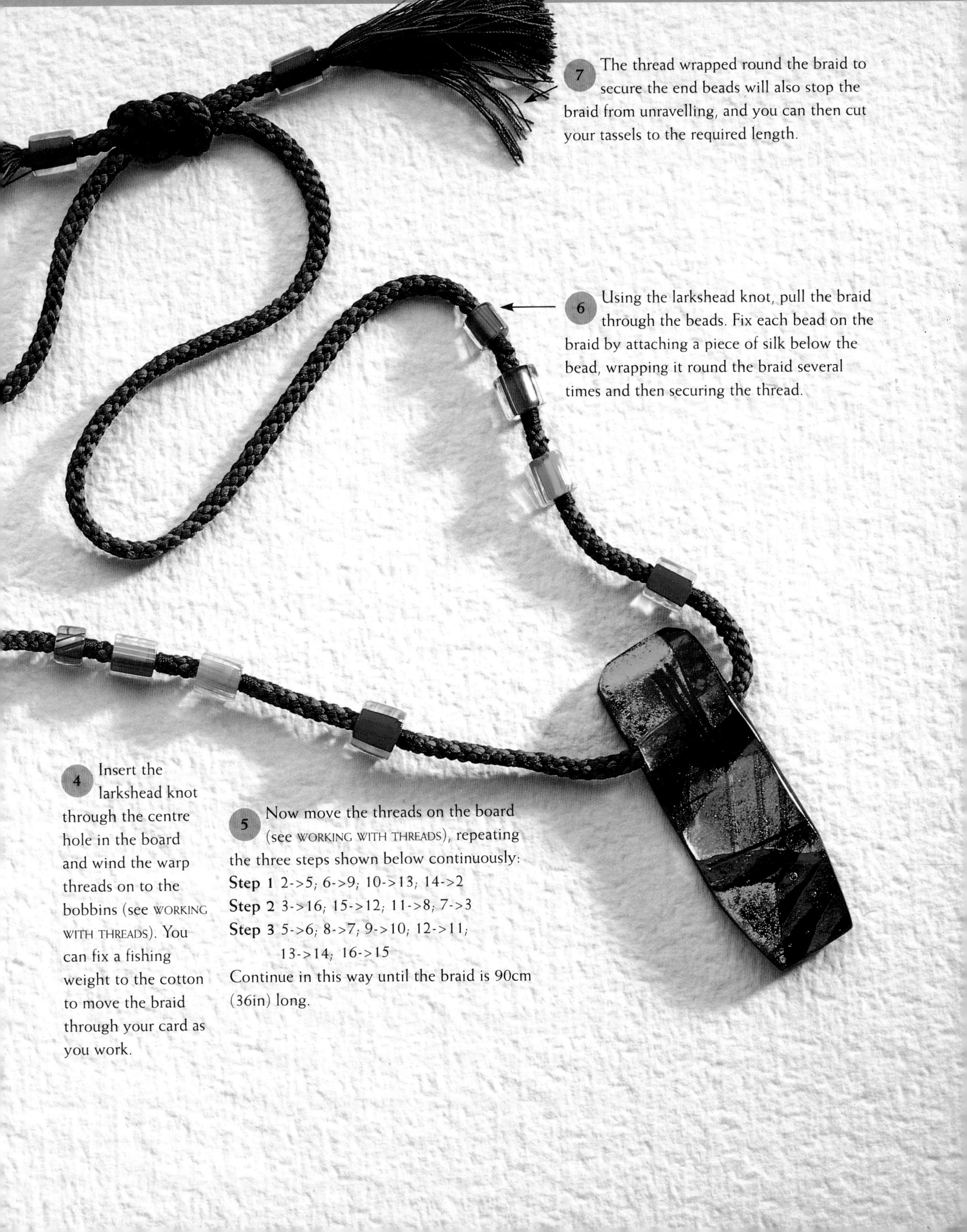

7 The thread wrapped round the braid to secure the end beads will also stop the braid from unravelling, and you can then cut your tassels to the required length.

6 Using the larkshead knot, pull the braid through the beads. Fix each bead on the braid by attaching a piece of silk below the bead, wrapping it round the braid several times and then securing the thread.

4 Insert the larkshead knot through the centre hole in the board and wind the warp threads on to the bobbins (see WORKING WITH THREADS). You can fix a fishing weight to the cotton to move the braid through your card as you work.

5 Now move the threads on the board (see WORKING WITH THREADS), repeating the three steps shown below continuously:

Step 1 2->5; 6->9; 10->13; 14->2

Step 2 3->16; 15->12; 11->8; 7->3

Step 3 5->6; 8->7; 9->10; 12->11; 13->14; 16->15

Continue in this way until the braid is 90cm (36in) long.

PERUVIAN COLLAR

THIS HAND-WOVEN COLLAR OF RICHLY COLOURED PERUVIAN BEADS FEATURES A DELICATE PATTERN OF DROP BEADS SUSPENDED FROM THE CENTRE. THE COLLAR IS FINISHED WITH CHAIN SO ITS LENGTH IS ADJUSTABLE.

YOU WILL NEED
Round-nosed pliers
Necklace pliers
Wire cutters
2 fine needles

FOR THE NECKLACE
The basic items listed below and the beads shown opposite:
1 small Inca pendant *idolus*
21 50mm (2in) eye pins
7 3mm silver-plated balls
9 7mm (¼in) silver-plated jump rings
2 silver-plated calottes
Length of silver-plated chain
1 silver-plated hook/silver-plated jewellery wire to make one
4m (4⅓yd) black polyester thread
149 black rocailles size 0/7

1 First make the hanging pieces in the same way as straight earrings (see USING WIRE). It is important to make your loop face in the same direction as the ready-made loop so the necklace will hang well. There are 19 hanging pieces in total.

2 Link the hanging pieces together with seven of the jump rings, as shown in the illustration. Make sure that all your loops face in the same direction. You will have two drop pieces left over.

3 Cut two 2m (6ft 6in) lengths of the polyester thread and thread it on your needles. Knot the ends of the threads together, and thread both strands through one rocaille, a 5mm bead and another rocaille. Separate the threads and handweave through rocailles and 5mm beads (see BEADWORK), into striped tube beads.

4 Continue in this way until you have threaded seven tubes, then pick up the first hanging piece. Thread it on the bottom thread between the 5mm black bead and the rocaille before you thread up through the next striped tube (the eighth).

5 Between the ninth and tenth tubes pick up the first linked pattern piece between the second and third rocaille.

50
5MM BLACK BEADS

6 Continue until you have reached the twelfth tube bead (striped), then add the second hanging piece between the first and second rocaille.

8 Before you finish off the threads, use your last eye pin to hang the little Inca pendant from the loop at the bottom. Thread the beads, then work the eye pin up through the middle of the central tube bead. Put more beads on the top of the eye pin, and very neatly roll its top.

9 Now finish your threads. First make sure the weaving is tight and even, then put on a calotte (see FINISHING).

7 The fourteenth bead is the centre of the collar, after this you can repeat the weaving and pick up the hanging pieces in the same way as on the other side of your work.

10 Cut the threads as neatly as possible.

11 Using the last jump rings, attach a 14cm (5½in) length of chain to one side and a 7cm (2¾in) length to the other. Put the hook on the shorter piece of chain. It needs to be able to slip through the links of the chain so you can wear the collar at different lengths.

13
PATTERNED DROP BEADS

23
STRIPED CERAMIC TUBE BEADS

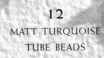

12
MATT TURQUOISE TUBE BEADS

The French
were famous for
their imitation pearls
and along with the Venetians,
made the tiny beads known as
rocailles or seed beads. Austria was famous
for its crystal glass beads, perfected by Daniel Swarovski,
Germany for the cutting and polishing of stone beads in
Idar-Oberstein. The British manufactured glass beads,
especially the "square cut" beads, used in the lace trade.

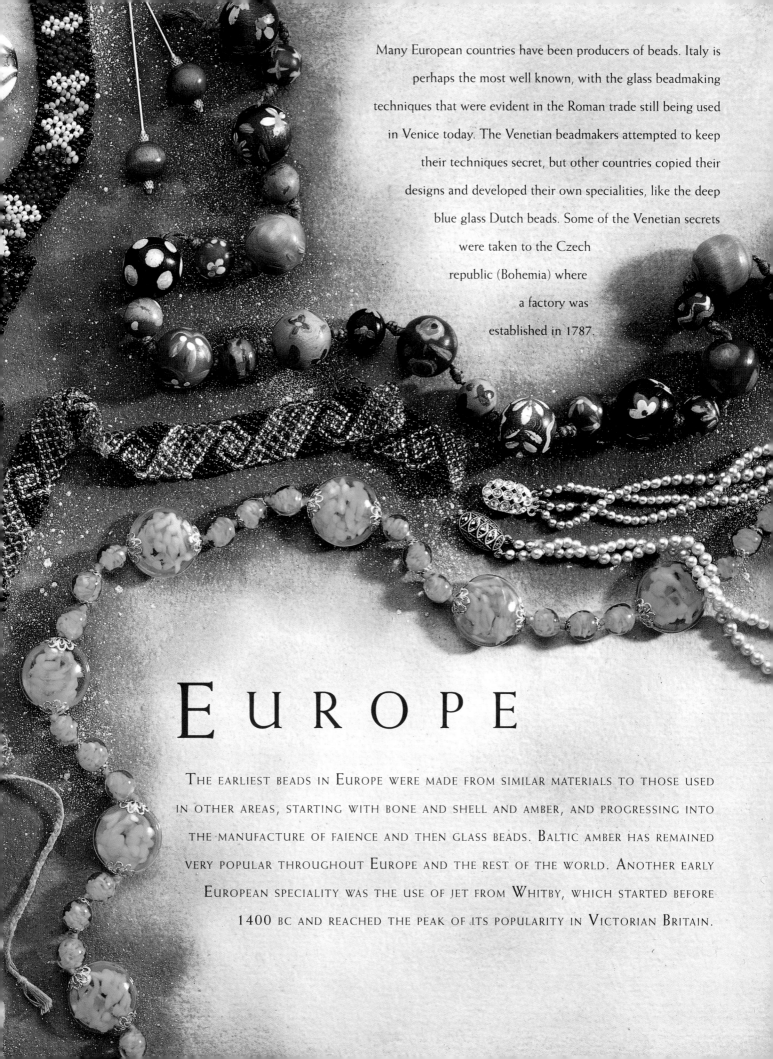

Many European countries have been producers of beads. Italy is perhaps the most well known, with the glass beadmaking techniques that were evident in the Roman trade still being used in Venice today. The Venetian beadmakers attempted to keep their techniques secret, but other countries copied their designs and developed their own specialities, like the deep blue glass Dutch beads. Some of the Venetian secrets were taken to the Czech republic (Bohemia) where a factory was established in 1787.

EUROPE

THE EARLIEST BEADS IN EUROPE WERE MADE FROM SIMILAR MATERIALS TO THOSE USED IN OTHER AREAS, STARTING WITH BONE AND SHELL AND AMBER, AND PROGRESSING INTO THE MANUFACTURE OF FAIENCE AND THEN GLASS BEADS. BALTIC AMBER HAS REMAINED VERY POPULAR THROUGHOUT EUROPE AND THE REST OF THE WORLD. ANOTHER EARLY EUROPEAN SPECIALITY WAS THE USE OF JET FROM WHITBY, WHICH STARTED BEFORE 1400 BC AND REACHED THE PEAK OF ITS POPULARITY IN VICTORIAN BRITAIN.

CROWNING JEWELS

THIS PEARL AND DIAMANTÉ SET OF BROOCH, PIN, AND AN ELEGANT CHOKER THAT DOUBLES AS A TIARA

MIGHT HAVE GRACED AN EDWARDIAN EUROPEAN COURT – BUT WOULD LOOK JUST AS GOOD IN A

1990s DISCOTHÈQUE!

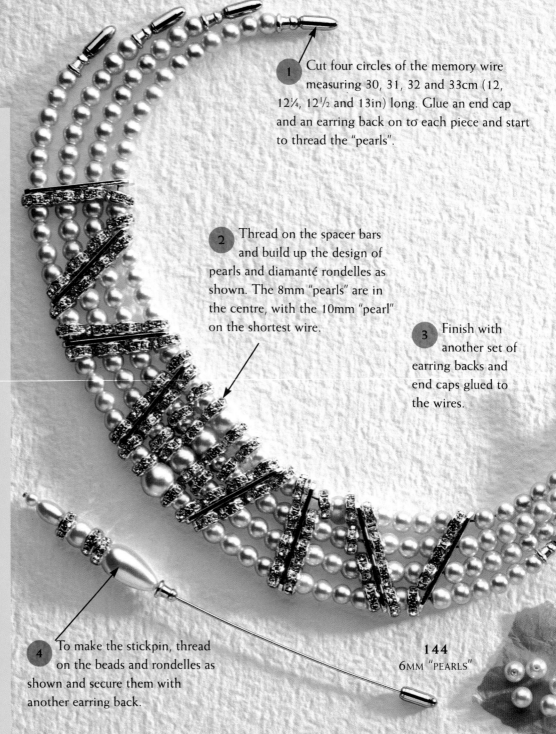

YOU WILL NEED
Round-nosed pliers
Wire cutters
Scissors
Glue

FOR THE CHOKER
The basic items listed
  below and the
  beads shown
  opposite:
8 x 4-hole spacer
  bars
126cm (50in)
  memory wire
8 end caps
8 earring backs

FOR THE STICKPIN
1 x 13cm (5in)
  stick-pin
1 end cap
1 earring back
3 diamanté rondelles
1 x 16 x 10mm
  "pearl" drop
1 x 10mm oval
  "pearl"
1 x 8mm "pearl"
1 x 4mm "pearl"

1 Cut four circles of the memory wire measuring 30, 31, 32 and 33cm (12, 12¼, 12½ and 13in) long. Glue an end cap and an earring back on to each piece and start to thread the "pearls".

2 Thread on the spacer bars and build up the design of pearls and diamanté rondelles as shown. The 8mm "pearls" are in the centre, with the 10mm "pearl" on the shortest wire.

3 Finish with another set of earring backs and end caps glued to the wires.

4 To make the stickpin, thread on the beads and rondelles as shown and secure them with another earring back.

144
6MM "PEARLS"

11 Separate the threads, working one down the side of the spacer bar, adding "pearls" and coming back through all but the bottom one, which will secure the others.

10 Bring the tiger tail back through the pattern of the clasp to secure it and work back to the bottom of the clasp again.

12 Put a "pearl" and a rondelle on the second thread and join it to the other piece of tiger tail with either a crimp, or a knot and a little glue. To finish, glue a brooch back to the clasp.

9 Work up through the loops in the same way. Add a "pearl" and a rondelle and thread through the diamanté clasp.

5 Start the brooch by making the hanging pieces, threading "pearls" and rondelles on to the head pins.

8 Cut 40cm (16in) of tiger tail and fold it in half. Put the middle round one of the loops, and thread down between the loops, adding a pearl between each. Come out of the bottom pearl and work back into the others on this side to hold them.

6 Make five figure 8 findings (see USING WIRE) and hang the pieces from them.

7 Cut four lengths of wire approximately 35, 45, 50 and 55mm (1¼, 1¾, 2 and 2¼in) long, roll one end and then thread the spacer bars with the beads and rondelles between them, and roll the other end. As you thread the bottom row add the hanging pieces.

FOR THE BROOCH
Half a diamanté clasp
1 brooch back
Tiger tail
2 4-hole spacer bars
40cm (16in) 0.8mm silver-plated wire
2 50mm (2in) head pins
3 38mm (1½in) head pins
17 diamanté rondelles
1 10mm "pearl"
17 8mm "pearls"
15 6mm "pearls"
6 4mm "pearls"
5 5mm "pearls"

1
10MM "PEARL"

3
8MM "PEARLS"

70
8MM DIAMANTE RONDELLES

ANCIENT AND MODERN

THESE STRIKING, RICHLY-COLOURED NECKLACES COMBINE METALLIZED PLASTIC
BEADS FROM ITALY AND GLASS BEADS FROM AUSTRIA. THE MANUFACTURE OF
PLASTIC BEADS HAS UNDERGONE A HUGE REVIVAL IN RECENT YEARS, PROVIDING
A GREAT SOURCE OF INSPIRATION TO JEWELLERY DESIGNERS. IN CONTRAST,
CRYSTAL GLASS BEADS HAVE BEEN MADE IN AUSTRIA SINCE THE LATTER HALF OF
THE NINETEENTH CENTURY BY A COMPANY FOUNDED BY DANIEL SWAROVSKI,
WHO INVENTED A MACHINE TO CUT GLASS BEADS. SWAROVSKI BEADS HAVE
BEEN HIGHLY REGARDED
EVER SINCE.

YOU WILL NEED
Necklace pliers
Round-nosed pliers
Scissors
Glue

FOR THE BRONZE AND
GOLD NECKLACE
The basic items listed
below and the
beads shown
opposite:
1m (39in) nylon line
1 small copper-plated
sprung clasp
2 oval copper-plated
jump rings
2 small copper-plated
calotte crimps
3 22mm gold-lined
beads
10 8mm coppered
beads
10 coppered barrel
beads
6 coppered fletcha
beads
10 small coppered
fletcha beads

FOR THE BRONZE AND
GOLD EARRINGS
2 gilt-plated ear
wires
2 50mm (2in) gilt-
plated head pins
2 10mm topaz facet
beads
2 14mm gold-lined
beads
4 8mm coppered
beads
8 coppered segments

18
14MM GOLD-
LINED BEADS

10
10MM TOPAZ
FACET BEADS

2
COPPERED RINGED
BARREL BEADS

4
COPPERED RIBBED
BEADS, WITH
LARGE HOLE

1 Cut 1m (39in) of the nylon line for each necklace, and make a firm knot in one end. Put a drop of glue on the knot, and when it is dry, put a calotte over it.

2 Thread the beads as shown, and knot again at the other end. Repeat the procedure to attach the calotte.

3 Use two oval jump rings to attach the fastener to the bronze and gold necklace; the red and gold necklace has a round jump ring and a split ring.

4 Make the bronze and gold earrings as simple straight earrings (see USING WIRE).

5 To make the red and gold earrings, thread the bottom beads on to the head pins and roll the tops. Open the bottom loops of the eye pins to attach the head pins. Thread the top beads on to the eye pins, roll the tops and attach the ear wires.

FOR THE RED AND GOLD NECKLACE
The basic items listed below and the beads shown opposite:
1m (39in) nylon line
1 small gilt-plated sprung clasp
1 5mm gilt-plated split ring
1 5mm gilt-plated jump ring
2 gilt-plated calotte crimps
4 gold milled beads
8 golden zig-zag beads
2 elliptical golden beads

FOR THE RED AND GOLD EARRINGS
2 gilt-plated ear wires
2 50mm (2in) gilt-plated head pins
2 10mm (½in) gilt-plated eye pins
2 amber egg-shaped beads
4 patterned golden flat beads
4 3mm golden balls
2 10mm topaz facet beads

6
AMBER EGG-SHAPED BEADS

AMBER CUSHION BEAD

8
GLASS TOFFEE BAROQUE BEADS

8
GOLD PATTERNED HEXAGON BEADS

14
SMALL ROUND GOLDEN BAROQUE BEADS

EDWARDIAN CHOKER

THIS CHOKER WAS INSPIRED BY EDWARDIAN PORTRAITS. YOU CAN IMAGINE IT AROUND THE NECK OF AN EDWARDIAN SOCIETY BEAUTY, AS WELL AS WEARING IT YOURSELF. IT IS MADE ON A LOOM, AND THE COMBINATION OF THE DESIGN AND THE COLOURS PRODUCES A WONDERFULLY RICH EFFECT.

1 For the quickest results, it helps to draw the design on graph paper before youstart to work on the loom. The choker has 134 rows (including the tag) and is 12 rocailles wide. It measures approximately 40cm (15¾in) long. If you draw up the design first you can lengthen or shorten it to suit.

4 There are 25 strands of fringe, and the length increases until there are 19 rocailles on the central one. They then decrease again to the other side of the fringing.

YOU WILL NEED
A bead loom
Beading needles
Scissors
Graph paper

FOR THE NECKLACE
The basic items listed
  below and the
  beads shown
  opposite:
Brown polyester
  thread

2 Thread the loom (see LOOM WORK) and work the first two rows. Then make the "eye" for the fastener by working half rows for four rows. (Work up one side, thread back down and repeat on the other.)

3 Continue to weave in pattern for another 52 rows, then add the first piece of fringing. Put five rocailles on your thread (from top to bottom gold, cream, bronze, gold, cream) and bring your needle back through the first four so that the fifth (cream) turns sideways and holds the fringe at the bottom. The needle goes back into the weaving to complete the row as usual.

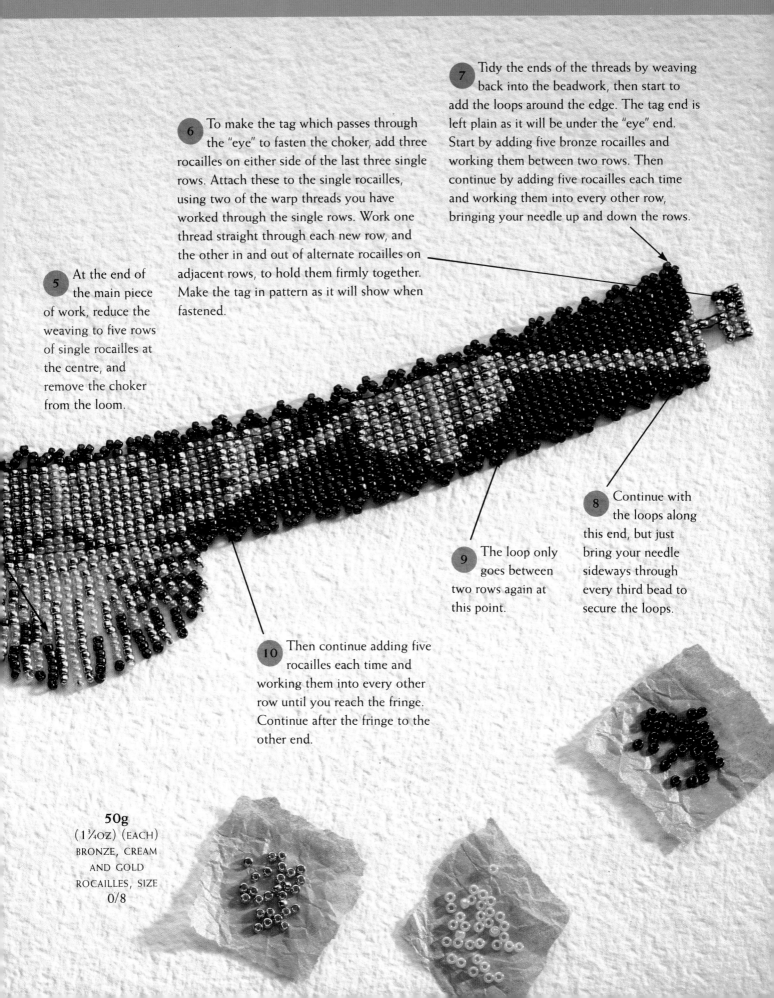

7 Tidy the ends of the threads by weaving back into the beadwork, then start to add the loops around the edge. The tag end is left plain as it will be under the "eye" end. Start by adding five bronze rocailles and working them between two rows. Then continue by adding five rocailles each time and working them into every other row, bringing your needle up and down the rows.

6 To make the tag which passes through the "eye" to fasten the choker, add three rocailles on either side of the last three single rows. Attach these to the single rocailles, using two of the warp threads you have worked through the single rows. Work one thread straight through each new row, and the other in and out of alternate rocailles on adjacent rows, to hold them firmly together. Make the tag in pattern as it will show when fastened.

5 At the end of the main piece of work, reduce the weaving to five rows of single rocailles at the centre, and remove the choker from the loom.

8 Continue with the loops along this end, but just bring your needle sideways through every third bead to secure the loops.

9 The loop only goes between two rows again at this point.

10 Then continue adding five rocailles each time and working them into every other row until you reach the fringe. Continue after the fringe to the other end.

50g (1¾OZ) (EACH) BRONZE, CREAM AND GOLD ROCAILLES, SIZE 0/8

GERMAN WOODEN BEAD SET

THIS COLOURFUL SET IS GREAT FUN TO MAKE. THE TECHNIQUES ARE QUITE SIMPLE, THE EMPHASIS BEING ON THE VARIETY OF COLOURS AND SHAPES. THE BEADS ARE MADE BY A GERMAN TOY MANUFACTURER, SO IT SEEMS A GOOD IDEA TO GET THE CHILDREN TO HELP MAKE THE JEWELLERY.

YOU WILL NEED
Round-nosed pliers
Necklace pliers
Wire cutters
File
Needle
Scissors

FOR THE NECKLACE
The basic items listed
  below and the
  beads shown
  opposite:
Hook and jump ring
  or 1.2mm silver-
  plated wire
75cm (30in) thick
  black thread
34 large flat black
  washer beads
6 flat square beads
2 large blue washer
  beads
6 8mm round pink
  beads
5 large flat red
  washer beads

FOR THE BRACELET
25cm (10in) 1.2mm
  silver-plated wire
  (less if you use a
  ready-made hook)
24 small flat washer
  beads
16 large flat washer
  beads
3 green cubes
2 small blue cubes
2 flat square beads

1 Cut the thread to the required length and thread the beads as shown, or to your design.

48
SMALL FLAT
WASHER BEADS

60
BLACK LICE BEADS

2
12MM ROUND
PINK BEADS

6
SMALL BLUE CUBES

2 At the end of both sides knot the thread on to the hook and jump ring (see FINISHING). If you are making your own hook (see USING WIRE). Thread the loose end of the thread on a needle and work it back down the beads.

EARRINGS

1 Thread a silver-plated ball onto a 50mm (2in) eye pin, followed by the wooden beads. Clip the top of the eye pin a little, and roll it.

2 Open the bottom loop on the 25mm (1in) eye pin sideways and hook it into the finished one. Thread the rest of the beads. Roll the top into a loop and add the ear wire. Repeat for the other earring.

BRACELET

1 Cut 20cm (8in) of wire, file one end and roll it into a loop. Thread on your beads.

2 Clip off any excess wire, leaving enough to match your first rolled end, file the end of the wire, and roll it into a loop. Attach your own hook, or a ready-made hook, to one of the loops.

FOR THE EARRINGS
4 silver-plated balls
2 50mm (2in) eye pins
2 25mm (1in) eye pins
2 ear wires
4 large flat black washer beads
4 small flat washer beads
2 flat square beads
2 green cubes
2 small blue cubes
10 black lice beads

6
GREEN CUBES

10
YELLOW WHEEL BEADS

BOHEMIAN CHAINS

THIS DELICATE SET HAS A WONDERFUL ASSORTMENT OF GLASS BEADS, INCLUDING THE PRETTILY PATTERNED LAMP BEADS, THAT ARE MAINLY FROM BOHEMIA, WORKED WITH SHORT PIECES OF CHAIN AND FRENCH ANTIQUE-STYLE ORNAMENTAL METAL PIECES INTO A LONG, LONG NECKLACE THAT CAN BE WOUND ROUND THE NECK SEVERAL TIMES. THE BRACELET IS ELEGANTLY SIMPLE, ADDING UP TO A VERY DRAMATIC COLLECTION.

1 Cut 40 pieces of chain, each approximately 4.5cm (1¾in), or eight links long.

2 Put a jump ring into both ends of each of the antiqued metal pieces.

3 Cut approximately 96 4cm lengths of wire to wire the beads. Some will require less, so trim the wires with your cutters before you roll the ends. Thread the wires through the beads.

4 When you have made loops in both ends of the bead pieces construct your necklace by opening the loops sideways and linking in the pieces of chain.

5 Open the jump rings on the antiqued metal pieces to attach the pieces of chain. Work until all the pieces are linked.

YOU WILL NEED
Round-nosed pliers
Wire cutters

FOR THE NECKLACE
The basic items listed
  below and the
  beads shown
  opposite:
180cm (6ft) of chain
8 antiqued metal
  pieces
16 3mm (⅒in) jump
  rings
Jewellery wire
8 7mm black faceted
  beads
4 black rocailles, size
  0/7

8
15 x 7MM GREY
GLASS "PEARLS"

8
11 x 8MM SOFT
GREEN AND SOFT
PINK LAMP
BEADS

24
4MM CREAM
GLASS "PEARLS"

BRACELET

1 Thread the beads for the bracelet in the same way as you did for the necklace, adding ornamental bead caps to the cream glass "pearls" and the pink lamp bead.

2 Link the pieces together with the 2mm ($^{1}/_{12}$in) jump rings, making two strands.

3 Attach the two strands to each large jump ring with two of the tiny jump rings.

4 Put the round jump ring and the trigger clasp on to the ends.

4
14 x 10MM BLUE
FACETED BEADS

4
7MM PURPLE
FACETED BEADS

24
5MM BLACK
FACETED BEADS

12
4MM BLACK
FACETED BEADS

FOR THE BRACELET

22 3mm (⅛in) jump rings

2 6 x 4mm (¼ x ⅛in) jump rings

1 5mm (¼in) jump ring

1 trigger clasp

12 ornamental bead caps

Jewellery wire

7 7mm black faceted beads

1 8mm black faceted bead

4 7mm purple faceted beads

2 14 x 10mm blue faceted beads

5 8mm cream glass "pearls"

4 3mm cream glass "pearls"

1 11 x 8mm pink lamp bead

GREEK CERAMICS

THE GREEKS MAKE A WONDERFUL RANGE OF CERAMIC BEADS, SOME WITH ELABORATE FLOWER DESIGNS, AND OTHERS, LIKE THOSE USED HERE, IN ANGULAR SHAPES AND SOFT SMUDGY COLOURS. MOST OF THE GREEK BEADS ARE DESIGNED TO BE USED WITH LEATHER, SO THIS PIECE USES RECTANGULAR CERAMIC TUBES AND LITTLE CERAMIC SQUARES THREADED ON LEATHER THONGS.

2 Cut three 30cm (12in) lengths of thonging. Thread on the rectangular tubes, with the small squares between them. In the centre of one thong, thread the hanging pieces between the small square beads.

1 Make the hanging pieces by cutting the hat-pin wires to the length of the beads plus 10mm (½in) to roll at the top to make loops large enough for the leather to go through. Take care when clipping the wires, they are very stiff and sharp when cut. Make sure you turn the ends in well so there are no rough edges.

YOU WILL NEED
Necklace pliers
Round-nosed pliers
Scissors
Wire cutters

FOR THE NECKLACE
The basic items listed
  below and the
  beads shown
  opposite:
9 hat-pin wires
110cm (1¼yd)
  leather thonging
1.2mm wire for hook,
  or ready-made
  hook
10 spring ends
2 7mm (¼in) jump
  rings
2 grey triple spacer
  beads

34
BLUE
RECTANGULAR
TUBES

15
GOLD MOTTLED
TUBES

5 Cut two 8cm (3¼in) lengths of thonging for the end pieces. Put a spring end on each end of the thongs, with the beads between them.

7 Finally add a ready-made hook, or one you have made yourself, (see USING WIRE) to one end of the necklace.

6 Link the pieces together at each end with a jump ring.

4 Finish each of the ends with a spring end, and link a jump ring through the spring ends.

3 Thread the thonging through the spacer beads, then continue with the rectangular tubes and small square beads.

30
GREY ROCAILLES,
SIZE 0/7

8
PLAIN GOLD
LARGER TUBES

55
SMALL GREY
SQUARES

COLOURFUL POLYMER

THESE NECKLACES ARE MADE FROM A SELECTION OF COLOURFUL AND INTRICATELY PATTERNED POLYMER CLAY BEADS HAND-MADE IN SCOTLAND. AVAILABLE IN A WIDE RANGE OF COLOURS, THE MATERIAL IS REASONABLY EASY TO HANDLE AND CAN BE FIRED IN AN ORDINARY OVEN OR EVEN IN BOILING WATER, SO IT IS POSSIBLE TO MAKE YOUR OWN BEADS, IF YOU PREFER, RATHER THAN BUYING THEM. HERE, BECAUSE THE DESIGN OF THE BEADS IS SO STRONG, THEY HAVE BEEN COMBINED WITH PLAIN BRASS WASHERS AND A FEW SMALL BRASS BEADS FROM GREECE IN SIMPLE DESIGNS STRUNG ON LEATHER THONGING, TO MAKE HEAVY, DRAMATIC JEWELLERY.

YOU WILL NEED
Necklace pliers

FOR THE NECKLACES
The basic items listed
   below and the
   beads shown
   opposite:
Large brass washers
Brass springs
Leather thonging in
   different colours
Round brass beads

PLAIN AND
PATTERNED
POLYMER CLAY
BEADS

TOP TWO NECKLACES

1 Decide on your arrangement of plain and patterned polymer clay beads, washers and brass beads. Ours is symmetrical.

2 Thread on all the beads and washers, then glue a bead at the end of each thong and tie a tight knot beside it. When worn, the necklaces are held in place by winding the end beads round each other.

BOTTOM TWO NECKLACES

1 Arrange the plain and patterned polymer clay beads, washers and brass beads symmetrically as before.

2 Thread on all the beads and washers, remembering to leave a gap between the beads and the fastener so the necklace won't be too stiff.

3 Loop the thong at one end, passing both ends of the loop through a brass spring. Squeeze the last coils of the spring in place with the necklace pliers.

4 At the other end put on two small beads, a toggle bead and another small bead, then tie a firm knot at the end of the thong.

LINDISFARNE TWIST

THIS IS A TRULY EUROPEAN DESIGN: THE HAND-EMBOSSED CERAMIC BEADS ARE A NEW ENGLISH DESIGN; THE SMALL SQUARE GLASS BEADS ARE LAMP-MADE "SQUARE CUTS" MUCH FAVOURED BY LACE-MAKERS AND ALSO MADE IN ENGLAND; THE ROCAILLES ARE FRENCH; AND THE MILLEFIORE GLASS BEADS ARE VENETIAN, OF THE WELL-KNOWN ROSETTA PATTERN.

1 Cut three lengths of thonging: 62cm (24in), 65cm (25in) and 68cm (26in) and thread the cylindrical ceramic beads into the centres of the pieces. Then thread the pink rocailles, smaller cylinders and round beads on either side for about 18cm (7in).

YOU WILL NEED
Necklace pliers
Scissors

FOR THE NECKLACE
The basic items listed
   below and the
   beads shown
   opposite:
6 leather spring ends
2m (6ft 6in) leather
   thonging
1 three-hole clasp
3.6m (4yd) 0.34
   gauge beading wire
5 23 × 20mm hand-
   embossed ceramic
   beads
10 6-7mm "square
   cuts"
Translucent cobalt
   and opaque pink
   rocailles, size 0/4
10 8mm Venetian
   millefiore beads

2 Cut about 120cm (4ft) of beading wire for each thong and wind a piece round a thong above the end pink rocailles, having made sure that you have centralized the beads on the thong. Leave a 20mm (¾in) "tail" on the wire before you wind it. You could tape the thongs together loosely at the other side for ease of working.

3 Thread the tiny 11/0 rocailles on to the wire and add the square cuts, alternated with the Venetian millefiore beads, before the central ceramic bead.

9 Clip off the ends of the thongs, and attach the spring ends to the fastener. Finally, clip off the "tails" on the lengths of wire

8 Make sure the beads are pushed down and neatly in place, and attach the spring ends to the ends of the thongs.

7 Add the translucent blue rocailles and ceramic beads to the length that you require at the ends of the thongs on both sides.

6 Position the two ceramic beads neatly above the wiring and over the three thongs at each side.

5 Make sure you are happy with the positioning of the strands and wiring, coil the wire securely round the other side of the thongs, again leaving a tail on the wire.

4 Wind the wire round the thong again, and pass it through the central bead. Do this with the other two strands, and then repeat on the other side.

16
20 x 7MM
HAND-EMBOSSED
CERAMIC TUBES

TRANSLUCENT
BLUE ROCAILLES,
SIZE 11/0

14
12MM ROUND
HAND-EMBOSSED
CERAMIC BEADS IN
2 DIFFERENT
PATTERNS

BLACK GLASS COLLAR

THIS CLASSIC DESIGN IS BASED ON THE JET COLLARS THAT WERE SO FASHIONABLE IN VICTORIAN TIMES.
THE FACETED BLACK BEADS ARE AUSTRIAN CUT GLASS, AND THEIR SPARKLE IS ENHANCED BY LITTLE GILT
BEAD CAPS. AN ORNATE DROPPER AND CHAIN FINISHES THE COLLAR.

YOU WILL NEED
Round-nosed pliers
Necklace pliers
Wire cutters

FOR THE NECKLACE
The basic items listed
   below and the
   beads shown
   opposite:
9 25mm (1in) gilt-
   plated eye pins*
13 38mm (1½in) gilt-
   plated eye pins*
1 50mm (2in) gilt-
   plated eye pins
6 gilt 3-hole spacer
   bars
2 gilt pretzel
   droppers
8.5cm (3½in) gilt
   chain
gilt bolt ring
105cm (41in) tiger
   tail
6 gilt-plated French
   crimps
32 4mm glass beads
115 6mm glass beads

*or cut down 22
   50mm (2in) eye
   pins

3 Attach a 3cm (1¼in) length of chain to one of the gilt droppers, and put a bolt ring on the other end of the chain.

4 Cut three 35cm (14in) pieces of tiger tail and attach them to the gilt dropper using French crimps. Put gilt-plated balls between the crimps and the dropper.

5 Thread towards the centre on all three strands, inserting the spacer bars as shown.

1 Make the hanging pieces as shown. All of these should be made in the same way as a simple straight earring (see USING WIRE), with the eye pin trimmed neatly above the beads and rolled.

2 Link the pieces together by opening the bottoms of the eye pins sideways and inserting the top loop from another piece. You can follow the arrangement from the illustration. Make sure all the loops are neatly closed.

8 Crimp the dropper on to the other side of the collar in the same way as you did the first one.

7 Reverse the pattern until you reach the other side of the collar.

6 Thread the central pattern picking up the hanging pieces on the bottom row. Start with a 6mm bead with one bead cap, then put on a 6mm bead with caps between each of the hanging pieces as they graduate towards the middle. Make sure all your loops face in the same direction.

9 Cut about 5.5cm (2in) of gilt chain and link it into this side of the dropper. The bolt ring can fasten into one of these links, at the required length.

16
8MM GLASS BEADS

26
5MM GLASS BEADS

32
3MM GILT-PLATED BALLS

108
6MM (¹/₄IN) GILT BEAD CAPS

India produces wonderful beads in
different metals and has a thriving
industry in glass beadmaking. Glass beads
have been made there since about 1000 BC, but during the
time of British rule large quantities of European beads were
imported into India, threatening their own manufacture,
although in recent years this has been reversed.

There is an abundance of beads in this area. Egypt is historically important for the faience beads, a forerunner to glass, used in ancient Egyptian jewellery and still made there. It is also the earliest known source of beadwork. Many beads traded from Europe and India into Africa and other Middle Eastern regions passed through Cairo. Metalworking techniques are skillfully used in the countries that we have grouped here, to make wonderful beads from silver, gold and base metals, along with lapis lazuli, coral, turquoise and amber.

MIDDLE EAST

IT WAS HARD TO SPLIT THE WORLD INTO FIVE REGIONS, CONTINENTS WOULD HAVE BEEN EASY GEOGRAPHICALLY, BUT NOT IN TERMS OF BEAD INFLUENCE AND INSPIRATION. OUR MIDDLE EASTERN AREA IS IMPORTANT BECAUSE THE PILGRIMS GOING TO MECCA STIMULATED THE TRADE IN BEADS, BOTH IN THE SPECIAL PRODUCTION OF BEADS FOR THAT MARKET AND THE MOVEMENT OF BEADS GENERATED BY THE PILGRIMAGES.

EASTERN INFLUENCE

THE BEADS USED FOR THIS ELEGANT CHOKER ARE A COOL MIXTURE OF AFGHANI LAPIS LAZULI AND CHINESE TURQUOISE, LINKED WITH RICH GOLDEN THAI BEADS AND GLOWING GARNETS FROM SRI LANKA.

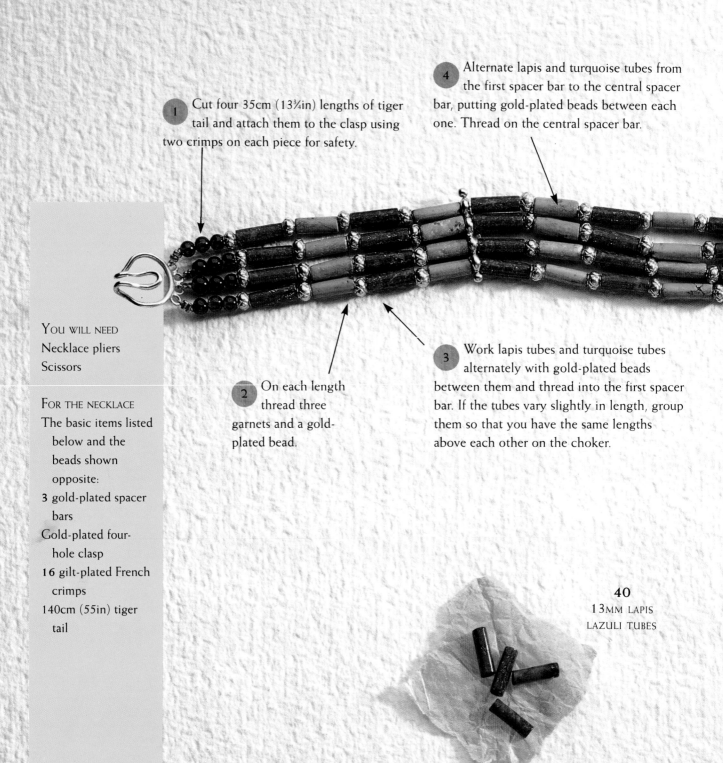

1 Cut four 35cm (13¾in) lengths of tiger tail and attach them to the clasp using two crimps on each piece for safety.

2 On each length thread three garnets and a gold-plated bead.

4 Alternate lapis and turquoise tubes from the first spacer bar to the central spacer bar, putting gold-plated beads between each one. Thread on the central spacer bar.

3 Work lapis tubes and turquoise tubes alternately with gold-plated beads between them and thread into the first spacer bar. If the tubes vary slightly in length, group them so that you have the same lengths above each other on the choker.

YOU WILL NEED
Necklace pliers
Scissors

FOR THE NECKLACE
The basic items listed below and the beads shown opposite:
3 gold-plated spacer bars
Gold-plated four-hole clasp
16 gilt-plated French crimps
140cm (55in) tiger tail

40
13MM LAPIS LAZULI TUBES

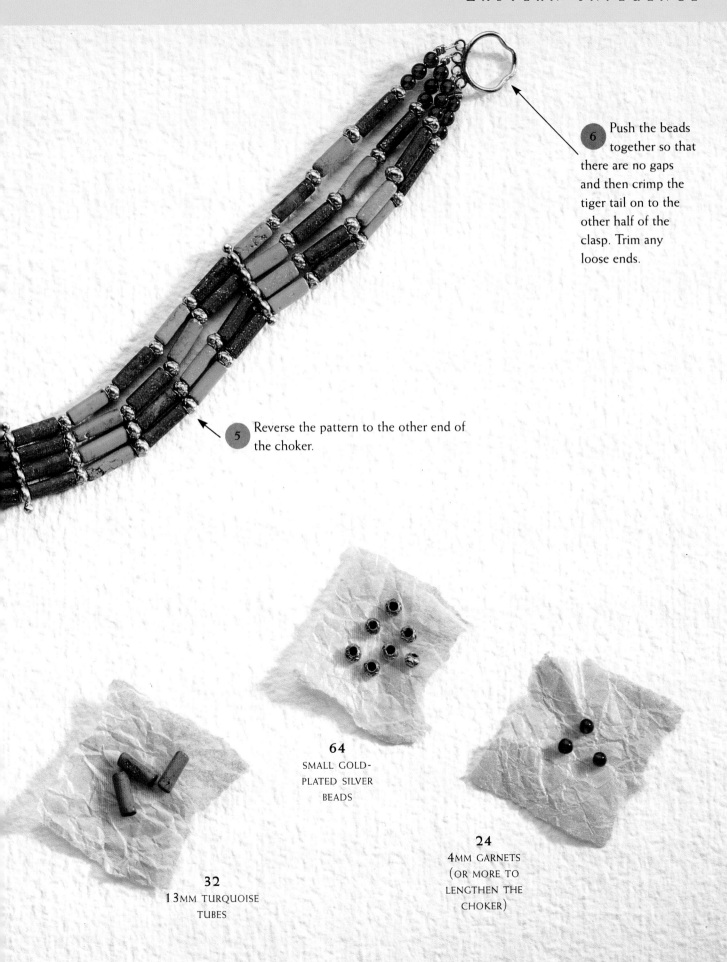

6 Push the beads together so that there are no gaps and then crimp the tiger tail on to the other half of the clasp. Trim any loose ends.

5 Reverse the pattern to the other end of the choker.

64
SMALL GOLD-
PLATED SILVER
BEADS

24
4MM GARNETS
(OR MORE TO
LENGTHEN THE
CHOKER)

32
13MM TURQUOISE
TUBES

MOSQUE BEADS

THE CENTRAL PENDANT OF THE NECKLACE AND ALL THE PATTERNED GLASS BEADS ARE MADE IN THE CZECH REPUBLIC FOR SALE TO PILGRIMS TO MECCA. THE SAME DESIGNS HAVE BEEN MADE FOR AT LEAST 150 YEARS. HERE THEY ARE COMBINED WITH OTHER GLASS BEADS IN A SIMPLE BUT STYLISH DESIGN TO HIGHLIGHT THE BEADS' FASCINATION.

YOU WILL NEED
Scissors
Needle
Glue
If making your own
hook and eye:
File
Round-nose pliers
Wire cutters

FOR THE NECKLACE
The basic items listed
   below and the
   beads shown
   opposite:
1 mosque pendant,
   red
2 spacer bars
7cm (2¾in) 0.8mm
   silver-plated wire/
   ready-made hook
   and eye
1m (39in) thick red
   polyester thread
20cm (8in) thin black
   polyester thread

1 Cut a short piece of thin black polyester thread and slide one of the black rocailles into its centre. Then, using it double, thread on the beads for the centre pattern in the design threading through the spacer bars as you work and finishing with one black rocaille.

2 Bring the double thread back through the spacer bar, separate the two ends of the thread beneath the bar and knot them firmly around the central thread. If possible put a tiny drop of glue on the knot before cutting the ends.

3 Put the mosque pendant in the middle of the red thread and start to thread up both sides working into the spacer bars.

29
SMALL CUBE
MOSQUE BEADS
(9 RED, 8 BLACK,
12 AMBER)

102
BLACK ROCAILLES,
SIZE 0/7

20
FACETED AMBER
GLASS BEADS

4 When you have threaded the beads, make knots to finish your pendant (see FINISHING). There are six knots between the beads and the hook and eye. The hook and eye shown here are hand made (see USING WIRE) but you could buy a ready-made fastener.

4 Work a split ring into the top links of both pieces of chain to join them, then hook the ear wire on to the split ring. Repeat for the second earring.

3 Cut two 2.5cm (1in) pieces of chain and hook them into the loops at each end of the horizontal eye pin.

EARRINGS

1 Thread the beads and spacer bars onto the eye pins. Roll the tops of the eye pins.

2 Take another eye pin, put on a black rocaille, then thread through the other pins, putting beads between them. Add another black rocaille and roll the end of this eye pin. Make sure that both loops are at the same angle.

6
OVAL RED
MOSQUE BEADS

33
5MM BLACK
GLASS BEADS

5
ROUND, FLAT,
AMBER MOSQUE
BEADS

FOR THE EARRINGS
8 50mm (2in) eye
   pins
10cm (4in) silver-
   plated chain
2 silver-plated ear
   wires
2 split rings
2 spacer bars
2 round, flat amber
   mosque beads
14 small cube
   mosque beads
   (2 red, 4 black,
   8 amber)
2 5mm black glass
   beads
34 black rocailles,
   size 0/7

EGYPTIAN COLLAR

DELICATE EGYPTIAN FAIENCE BEADS IN SOFT EARTH TONES AND BLUES SET WITH GOLD SPACER BARS AND
A PENDANT SCARAB MAKE A COLLAR FIT FOR CLEOPATRA.

1 Cut the tiger tail into three lengths: 40cm (16in), 36cm (14in), and 32cm (12in). Crimp (see FINISHING) the shortest length to the top of the dropper bar and start to thread the faience beads and the gilt-plated balls. Start with a ball and space three more among the beads. Faience beads come loosely strung from a bead supplier, so you can take off little sections and rethread them, but if any beads are uneven or thin, reject them.

2 After about 9cm (3½in) thread on the first spacer bar. Thread another 3.5cm (1¼in) of beads before the next spacer bar. The little gilt balls can be worked into the faience to suit your taste; only one is shown here.

YOU WILL NEED
Round-nosed pliers
Necklace pliers
Scissors
Varnish (optional)

FOR THE NECKLACE
The basic items listed
  below and the
  beads shown
  opposite:
1 scarab
1 gilt dropper bar
  with chain
2 50mm (2in) gilt eye
  pins
6 gilt-plated French
  crimps
108cm (43in) tiger
  tail

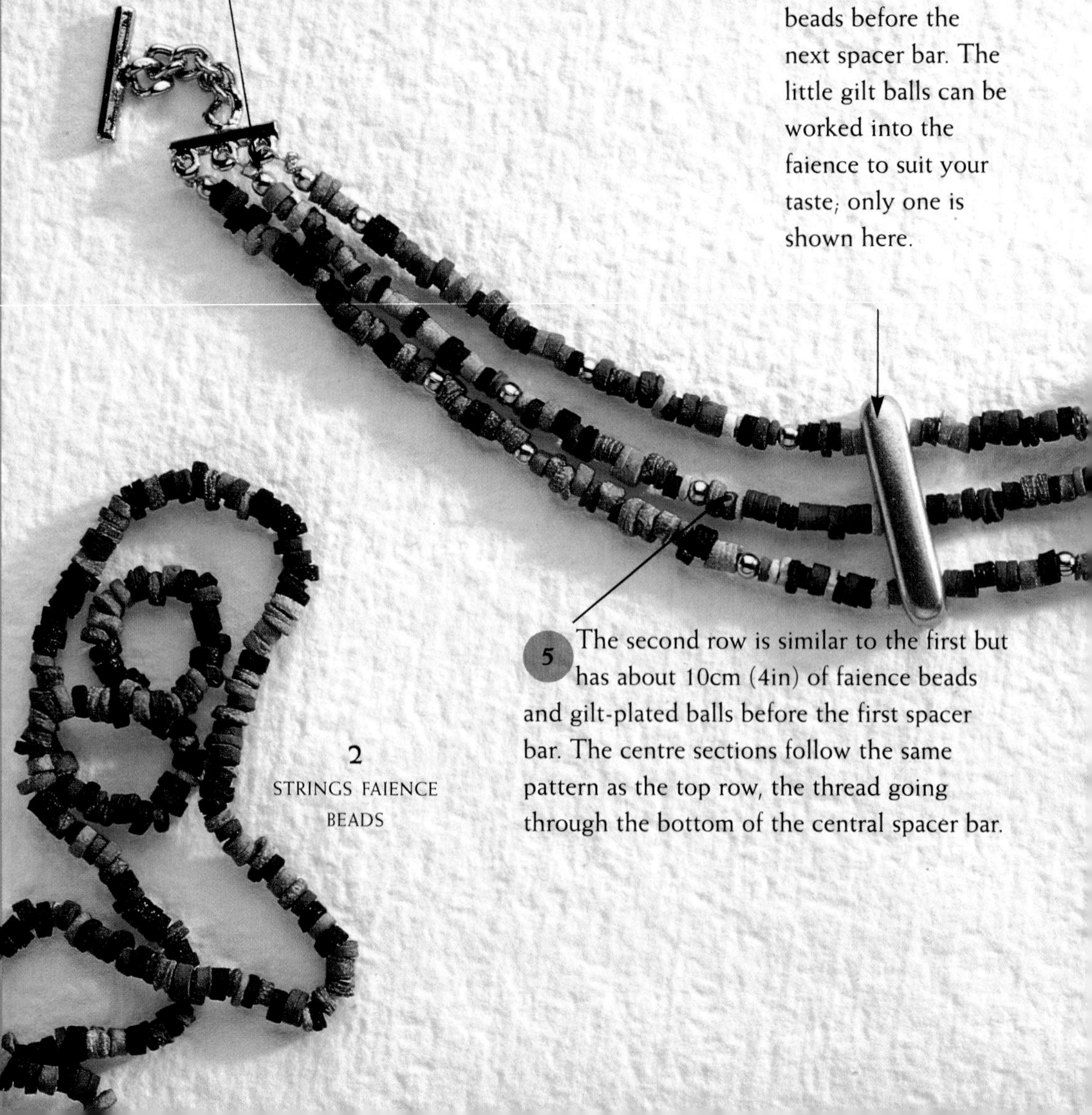

2
STRINGS FAIENCE
BEADS

5 The second row is similar to the first but has about 10cm (4in) of faience beads and gilt-plated balls before the first spacer bar. The centre sections follow the same pattern as the top row, the thread going through the bottom of the central spacer bar.

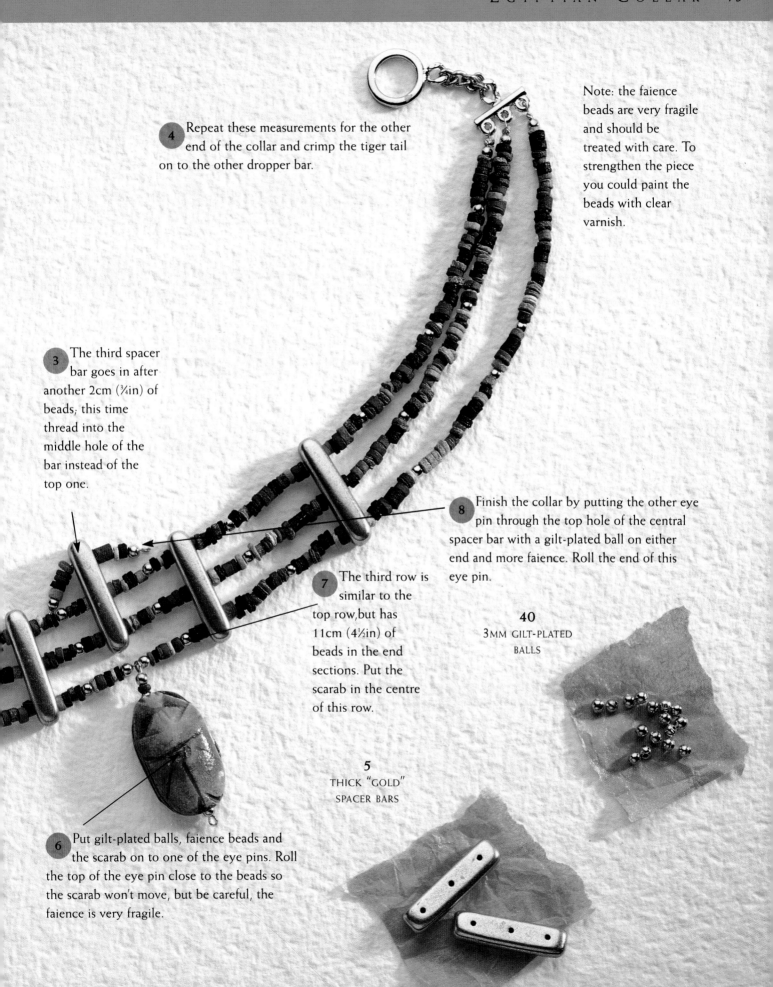

4 Repeat these measurements for the other end of the collar and crimp the tiger tail on to the other dropper bar.

Note: the faience beads are very fragile and should be treated with care. To strengthen the piece you could paint the beads with clear varnish.

3 The third spacer bar goes in after another 2cm (¾in) of beads; this time thread into the middle hole of the bar instead of the top one.

8 Finish the collar by putting the other eye pin through the top hole of the central spacer bar with a gilt-plated ball on either end and more faience. Roll the end of this eye pin.

7 The third row is similar to the top row, but has 11cm (4½in) of beads in the end sections. Put the scarab in the centre of this row.

40
3MM GILT-PLATED
BALLS

5
THICK "GOLD"
SPACER BARS

6 Put gilt-plated balls, faience beads and the scarab on to one of the eye pins. Roll the top of the eye pin close to the beads so the scarab won't move, but be careful, the faience is very fragile.

INDIAN AMETHYST AND SILVER

THE AMETHYSTS ARE HAND-CARVED IN SMALL VILLAGE WORKSHOPS IN RAJASTHAN, WHERE THE SILVER BEADS ARE ALSO MADE. THEY ARE THREADED SIMPLY BUT ASYMMETRICALLY, THE BEAUTY OF THE BEADS BEING OF PRIME IMPORTANCE IN BOTH NECKLACE AND EARRINGS.

YOU WILL NEED
Round-nosed pliers
Necklace pliers
Scissors

FOR THE NECKLACE
The basic items listed
  below and the
  beads shown
  opposite:
Strong nylon
  monofilament
2 French crimps
1 ornate clasp
2 5mm granulated
  silver beads
3 7mm granulated
  silver beads
6 14mm oblong
  silver beads
1 24mm off round
  decorated silver
  bead
4 20mm amethyst
  teardrop beads
2 10 x 22mm
  amethyst melon
  beads

THE NECKLACE
To make the necklace using these beads or similar ones, cut about 60cm (2ft) of nylon monofilament and thread from the middle of the necklace. As the design is asymmetrical, balance the shapes and sizes of the beads as you thread, checking how they hang together as you work.

7
10 X 14MM
AMETHYST MELON
BEADS

1
15 X 25MM
AMETHYST MELON
BEAD

2
20MM ROUND
SEAMED SILVER
BEADS

2
10 X 20MM
DECORATED
OBLONG SILVER
BEADS

2 Finish the necklace with crimps on either side of the fastener and trim the ends.

EARRINGS

To make the earrings, put the small silver balls and the teardrop beads on the head pins and roll the tops. Open the loops at the bottoms of the eye pins and link them into the head pins. Put on the remaining beads, and clip and roll the tops of the eye pins. Finally, put on the ear wires.

2
11 X 20MM PLAIT
DECORATION
SILVER BEADS

4
12MM SILVER
DISCS

10
5MM PLAIN AND
RIBBED SILVER
BEADS

1
6MM GRANULATED
SILVER BEAD

FOR THE EARRINGS

2 38mm silver-plated head pins

2 38mm silver-plated eye pins

2 ear wires

2 10 x 14mm amethyst melon beads

2 20mm amethyst teardrop beads

2 2mm ribbed silver beads

2 6mm granulated silver beads

2 3mm silver balls

MAGIC OF THE EAST

THE INSPIRATION FOR THIS PIECE COMES FROM SOME WONDERFUL OLD YEMENI JEWELLERY. WE'VE USED WHITE METAL BEADS TO MAKE IT MORE AFFORDABLE, BUT HAVE COMBINED THIS AND THE LITTLE TURQUOISE RESIN BEADS WITH SOME OLD NEPALESE SILVER FERTILITY CHARMS TO ADD TO THE IMPACT. YOU COULD ADD ANY INTERESTING SILVER OR METAL PIECES OF YOUR OWN IN THE CENTRES, TO CREATE YOUR OWN NECKLACE.

1 Cut your threads into graduating lengths and work from the centre of each strand. The white metal beads create an uneven effect because of their roughness, this adds to the "aged" effect. If you want to accentuate this try leaving the necklace in a steamy room to allow tarnishing.

2 Work the threads through the spacer bead, using a needle. Don't make the work too tight.

YOU WILL NEED
2m (6ft) thick
    polyester thread
12cm (5in) chain
1 hook and ring
2 large calottes
Necklace pliers
Large needle

FOR THE NECKLACE
The basic items listed
    below and the
    beads shown
    opposite:
3 assorted charms
218 metal discs

6 Repeat the finishing on this side and add the ring to the piece of chain here.

4 Squeeze a calotte over the knot. Open a link in the chain to attach it to the calotte.

3 With the threads together pass them through the last few beads on this side, and knot them together at the end. Use a needle in the knot to pull it close enough to the beads.

5 To add the hook, divide the chain into two pieces, by opening another link in the centre. (It may help to use two pairs of pliers if the chain is strong). Attach the hook.

156
WHITE METAL
BEADS

14
TURQUOISE RESIN
TUBES

2
3-HOLE SPACER
BEADS

55
TURQUOISE RESIN
OVAL BEADS

FROM THE MIDDLE EAST AND MIZORAM

THE BEADS IN THIS NECKLACE WILL BE MORE DIFFICULT TO FIND, BUT WE FELT THAT IT WOULD BE AN INSPIRATIONAL WAY TO SHOW WHAT CAN BE DONE WITH AN ASSORTMENT OF COLLECTED BEADS. OUR NECKLACE HAS OLD SILVER BEADS, A LITTLE CARNELIAN PENDANT AND SOME SMALL BONE BEADS FROM AFGHANISTAN. THE CENTRAL SQUARE BEAD IS A PUMTEK BEAD FROM MIZORAM IN INDIA. OLD PUMTEK BEADS ARE MADE OF OPALIZED WOOD AND ARE VERY COLLECTIBLE, BUT NEWER VERSIONS CAN ALSO BE FOUND. THE ROUNDER SILVER BEADS COME FROM IRAN, AS DO THE AMBER-COLOURED BEADS. THESE WERE SOLD AS AMBER, BUT ARE ACTUALLY MADE OF HORN.

YOU WILL NEED
3m (3¹/₄yd) coloured
 cord (from knitting
 supplier)
150cm (5ft) waxed
 thread
1 elaborate hook and
 ring
Needle
Glue (optional)

FOR THE NECKLACE
The basic items listed
below and the
beads shown
opposite:
4 Iranian silver beads
1 Pumtek bead
2 ornate horn beads
1 carnelian and silver
 pendant

2
YELLOW GLASS
BEADS

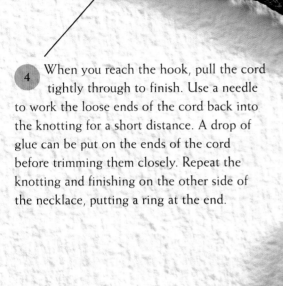

4 When you reach the hook, pull the cord tightly through to finish. Use a needle to work the loose ends of the cord back into the knotting for a short distance. A drop of glue can be put on the ends of the cord before trimming them closely. Repeat the knotting and finishing on the other side of the necklace, putting a ring at the end.

3 Knot the coloured cord to the waxed thread above the beads. Work the cord in square knots to within 2cm ($^{3}/_{4}$in) of the required length (see WORKING WITH THREADS). Knot the hook onto the waxed thread. Turn back the ends of the thread towards the beads. Continue the square knots over the ends of the thread to the hook.

2 Using two threads, work through the beads on this side. (Our ornate horn bead has two holes at the top, so the threads are separated here.)

1 Using the waxed thread double, thread from the centre of the necklace. Hang the pendant and bring all four strands through the central beads above it.

10
WHITE BONE
BEADS

7
HORN BEADS

4
AFGHAN SILVER
BEADS

INDIAN BAZAAR

THIS EXTRAVAGANT FANTASY IN BLUE, GREEN AND TURQUOISE FEATURES GLASS BEADS THREADED INTO
WHITE METAL BEADS, AND HUNG WITH CLUSTERS OF TINY INDIAN BELLS. YOU WILL NOT ONLY LOOK
WONDERFUL WEARING IT, YOU WILL SOUND WONDERFUL, TOO!

1 Put the bells on to the jump rings in groups of five. Put four of these jump rings on to the bottoms of four eye pins. Follow pattern with beads as shown. Clip off the top of the eye pins and roll tops.

3 Working from the middle, thread on the rocailles, 6mm beads, and flat round beads. Put the hanging bells and beads onto the bottom thread and work into the spacers as the pattern builds.

YOU WILL NEED
Round-nosed pliers
Necklace pliers
Scissors

FOR THE NECKLACE
The basic items listed below and the beads shown opposite:
4 3mm silver-plated balls
4 50mm (2in) silver-plated eye pins
8 7mm (¼in) silver-plated jump rings
2 silver-plated calottes
White metal fastener
4 large French crimps
1.8m (2yd) thick blue thread
152 iridescent purple rocailles, size 0/6

2 Cut three 60cm (24in) lengths of the blue thread and lay them out on your work-top. Thread one white metal spacer on to the middle of the threads. These spacers have two holes through them; put one thread through the top hole and two threads through the bottom hole.

40
TINY INDIAN
WHITE METAL
BELLS

4
WHITE METAL
BEADS

6 Work the same pattern of beads on the other side of the necklace. Before you use the French crimps on this side, push all the beads firmly back towards the other side so there are no gaps in the work. Check this again before you knot the threads.

4 Put on the last spacer bead and start to work the threads in together. Thread the top strand separately and the other two together. Work all three threads into a turquoise flat round bead.

7 Press a calotte firmly around the knot on both ends, and attach a fastener to each calotte (see FINISHING).

5 Put two French crimps on the second and third threads and press them with the pliers until the two strands are firmly connected. Cut off one of the threads, quite close to the crimps, and work a white metal bead over the remaining two threads, hiding the crimps beneath it. Work these two threads through the last three beads on this side and knot them.

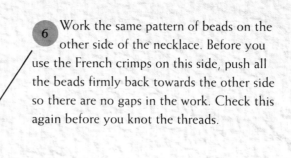

22
FLAT, ROUND,
14MM GLASS
BEADS
(10 GREEN,
6 BLUE,
6 TURQUOISE)

58
6MM GLASS
BEADS, ASSORTED
BLUES AND
GREENS

4
ROUND PATTERN
WHITE METAL
SPACER BEADS

3
HEART-SHAPED
WHITE METAL
SPACER BEADS

8
GLASS TEARDROP
BEADS, BLUE

INDIAN "COIN" NECKLACE

THESE "COINS" STAMPED "INDIA 1945" ARE HEAVY AND NEED TO BE USED SPARINGLY, SO THIS LONG DOUBLE NECKLACE IS IDEAL. THE BONE BEADS IN THE NECKLACE AND THE RUDRAKSHA SEEDS ARE ALSO FROM INDIA. THE LATTER, WHICH ARE ALSO CALLED "SIVA'S EYE" BEADS, ARE WORN BY THE FOLLOWERS OF LORD SIVA.

YOU WILL NEED
Round-nosed pliers
Needle

FOR THE NECKLACE
The basic items listed
below and the
beads shown
opposite:
2 Indian "coins"
0.8mm brass wire
4m (13ft) thick black
thread
10 long bone curve
and star beads
22 5mm black glass
beads
42 black rocailles
size 0/7

FOR THE EARRINGS
2 Indian "coins"
2 50mm (2in) gilt-
plated eye pins
2 gilt or gold ear
wires
0.8mm brass wire
2 long bone star
beads
4 black rocailles,
size 0/7

1 Start by wiring the coins so they will hang flat, (see USING WIRE). The brass wire is very springy and you need some strength to bend it.

2 Cut two pieces of black thread, one just over, and one just under 1m (39in) long. Position one of the "coins" in the middle of the longer piece. Thread the pattern of beads on both sides as shown ending with a rocaille.

3 Hang a "coin" on the shorter thread and work the same pattern of beads on to it, ending with a long bone star bead.

Earrings

Wire the "coins" and hang them in the loops at the bottom of the eye pins. Then thread the beads and turn the loops as in normal straight earrings. Put on the ear wires.

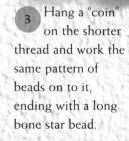

4 Work both the longer and shorter threads into a 5mm black bead on each side.

9 Work the buttonholing thread under the end left-hand glass bead, knot it firmly, and work the thread on under a few more beads before trimming off the end.

8 Using the newly joined thread, use buttonholing (see WORKING WITH THREADS) to bind across all the threads at the top of the necklace. Make sure the buttonholing covers everything underneath.

7 Lay the threads across the top of the necklace and knot the two sides together to give the required length of the finished piece.

5 Continue working both ends of thread through the beads in the sequence as before, but using a 5mm black bead instead of a rocaille between the larger beads.

6 Before you thread the last black 5mm bead on the right-hand side of the necklace, tie another 2m (6ft 6in) length of thread round both strands of the necklace, then thread the bead over this new thread as well as the existing ones.

12
LONG BONE STAR
BEADS

28
BONE STAR CUBE
BEADS

14
RUDRAKSHA
SEEDS, PAINTED
GOLD AND
BRONZE

RAJASTHAN NECKLACE

THIS HEAVY, DRAMATIC NECKLACE USES BLUE-GREEN CERAMIC BEADS FROM RAJASTHAN, INDIA, COMBINED
WITH SMALL, LUSTROUS BLUE AND GREEN GLASS BEADS AND DEEP BLUE
GLASS ONES. GLOWING WITH
RICH COLOUR, IT IS EASY TO MAKE,
BUT REQUIRES CAREFUL
THREADING AND COUNTING.

1 Cut a 30cm (12in) length of thread and loop it round one ceramic heart.

2 Add 17 rocailles to the outer thread, alternating blue and green beads. Centre these on the thread, then work both ends through a blue bead, a round ceramic bead and another blue bead. Separate the threads and work in pattern, joining and separating as you add the beads.

5 Put another 30cm (12in) thread around the inside of the first heart and repeat the pattern until the end of step 3, looping round the central heart again.

6 After the heart work as before and finish with another blue bead. Separate the threads again and put nine rocailles on each, again making temporary knots.

YOU WILL NEED
Scissors
Necklace pliers
Glue
Needle

FOR THE NECKLACE
The basic items listed
   below and the
   beads shown
   opposite:
3 ceramic hearts
2 large calottes
Fastener
5m (5½yd) thick blue
   polyester thread

3 Separate the threads and add a rocaille, a blue glass bead then six rocailles on each thread. Put another heart between these threads and then thread them together into a blue bead. Follow with seven rocailles on each thread, then work them back together into another blue bead.

4 Separate the threads again and follow the sequences as before. After the last ceramic bead add a blue bead, then separate the threads once more and thread seven rocailles on to each. Make temporary knots at the bottom of the threads.

7 Cut two 70cm (27½in) lengths of thread and put 13 rocailles, alternating blue and green, on to the middle of each. Loop each around the top of the first heart, join the threads, and pass each double into two blue beads. Then thread all four ends into an oval ceramic bead.

8 Separate the threads again and work them either double or singly into the different beads.

9 Repeat this pattern on the other double thread and then pass all four threads into another oval ceramic bead.

10 Above this bead the threads work together into a blue bead and singly into five rocailles. Do this six times on both double threads, then work the four threads into one blue glass bead.

11 Finish this side by knotting and using a calotte (see FINISHING).

12 Repeat all these steps on this side of the necklace. When both sides are finished, attach the fastener to the calottes.

13 When you have checked your work, undo your temporary knots and re-knot them one by one, using a needle (see FINISHING). When the knots are close and neat, put a drop of glue on them to give extra security, and trim the ends.

112
5MM BLUE GLASS BEADS

8
LARGE OVAL CERAMIC BEADS

28
ROUND CERAMIC BEADS

708
BLUE AND GREEN GLASS ROCAILLES, SIZE 0/6

FAR EAST

THE FAR EAST EVOKES VISIONS OF JADE AND PEARLS SPREADING INTO THE REST OF THE WORLD ALONG WITH THE SILKS AND SPICES. THE OLD TRADING ROUTES MOVED NORTH THROUGH RUSSIA, AND EAST THROUGH SOUTH AMERICA BRINGING THESE RICHES TO THE REST OF THE WORLD, WITH A WEALTH OF OTHER BEADS. THE ROUTES MAY HAVE CHANGED IN MODERN TIMES BUT THE DIVERSITY OF BEADS FROM THE AREA REMAINS AS REWARDING AS EVER.

Ceramic beads are made in Thailand and many semi-precious beads are traded in Bangkok. The lac and metal beads using Khmer skills, now mainly made in Thailand, are famous. The Philippines produce decorated wooden, shell and coral beads. Indonesia makes beads using natural materials and glass, and there are the beautiful silver beads from Bali.

The Chinese have been making beads from glass for about three thousand years. They were important both within Chinese society, and in its export trade. Enamelling was introduced from the West, but the Chinese are masters in making exquisite cloisonné enamelled beads, as well as beautifully carved cinnabar beads. Their strong traditions of hand painting and porcelain manufacture have resulted in fine porcelain beads. The Japanese also have a long tradition of bead making, the most well known being the highly decorated Ojime.

CHINESE CINNABAR

THE LITTLE SILVER-PLATED FIGURES ADD A TOUCH OF ECCENTRICITY TO THE RICH MIXTURE OF RUST

COLOURS IN THIS DESIGN WHILE THE JASPAR DONUTS COMPLEMENT THE COLOURS PERFECTLY.

TRUE CINNABAR BEADS ARE MADE FROM MANY COATS OF LACQUER, COLOURED WITH THE RED CINNABAR

DYE, AND THEN CARVED.

YOU WILL NEED
Round-nosed pliers
Necklace pliers
Needle

FOR THE NECKLACE
The basic items listed
  below and the
  beads shown
  opposite:
1 silver-plated
  pendant
2 calottes
1 fastener
2+ metres (6ft 6in+)
  thick red thread

FOR THE EARRINGS
2 silver-plated figures
2 50mm (2in) eye
  pins
2 silver-plated ear
  wires
2 round cinnabar
  beads
4 dark grey rocailles,
  size 0/7

1 Cut two 1m (39in) lengths of the thread (enough to trim the ends as you work). Put both through the pendant and position it in the middle of the threads.

2 Work all the threads through a bamboo bead, then separate them. The following instructions apply to both sides. Continue to thread as shown, using the two strands separately and together. You may need a needle to thread through the figure.

8
ROUND CINNABAR
BEADS

3
HEAVY PLASTIC
"BAMBOO" BEADS

6
OVAL CINNABAR
BEADS

2
JASPAR "DONUTS"

3 At this point, put five rocailles on each thread, place the donut between the threads and join the threads again through a tile bead.

5 Continue to add the beads following the pattern shown.

4 Separate again, add five more rocailles on each thread at the other side of the donut, and join the threads by passing them through a round cinnabar bead.

6 Finish with both threads in a tile bead, then push all the beads towards the pendant and knot the threads. Use a calotte (see FINISHING), and hook on a fastener.

EARRINGS
To make the earrings, thread a figure and the beads on to each eye pin. Roll the top and add the ear wire.

142
DARK GREY
ROCAILLES,
SIZE 0/7

72
BROWN TILE
BEADS

6
SILVER-PLATED
FIGURES

CHINESE TWIST

THESE LOVELY BLUE AND WHITE PORCELAIN BEADS PATTERNED WITH TRADITIONAL DESIGNS ARE PROBABLY THE MOST FAMILIAR OF THE CHINESE BEADS. IN THIS NECKLACE THREE STRANDS OF BEADS IN DIFFERENT SHAPES AND SIZES ARE TWISTED TOGETHER TO MAKE A THICK ROPE. THE MATCHING EARRINGS ARE HEAVY AND DRAMATIC.

1 Cut the thread into three equal lengths and lay out the design. Use smaller beads at the sides and progress into the bigger ones. Try twisting the threads as you work to see how the beads lie together.

YOU WILL NEED
Round-nosed pliers
Necklace pliers
Scissors

FOR THE NECKLACE
The basic items listed
 below and the
 beads shown
 opposite:
1 8mm (⅜in) jump
 ring
160cm (63in) thick
 blue polyester
 thread
12 French crimps
2 pairs Thai silver
 coiled hook and
 eye clasps

185
PURPLE
ROCAILLES,
SIZE 0/6

33
6MM STRIPED
PORCELAIN BEADS

36
6MM PATTERNED
PORCELAIN BEADS

3 Gently squeeze one end of the clasp around the jump ring to hold it in place. Twist the necklace several times before wearing it.

4 Put the beads onto the eye pins. Link the rolled top of the small eye pin into the bottom loop on the central eye pin. Roll the tops of the other eye pins and open their loops sideways to hang them into the loops on the "eye" pieces of the coiled clasps. Ensure all loops are facing the same way. Finally, add the ear wires.

2 At each end of each thread, use two crimps with a rocaille between them and thread two "hook" pieces of the clasps, crossing the middle and bottom rows before crimping them. When everything is neatly in place squeeze the crimps.

12
FLAT ROUND
PORCELAIN BEADS

12
OVAL PORCELAIN
BEADS

45
6MM BLUE BEADS
12
6MM CLEAR
RAINBOW BEADS

FOR THE EARRINGS
6 50mm (2in) eye
  pins
2 25mm (1in) eye
  pins
2 ear wires
6 oval porcelain
  beads
2 flat round porcelain
  beads
4 6mm patterned
  porcelain beads
6 6mm striped
  porcelain beads
2 6mm blue beads
28 purple rocailles,
  size 0/6

PHOENIX RISING

SHOWN MAINLY TO BE INSPIRATIONAL, THE BEADS AND CENTREPIECE IN THIS AMAZING NECKLACE ARE MADE FROM POLYMER CLAY. WE HAVE SHOWN YOU HOW TO MAKE BEADS IN THE TECHNIQUES SECTION, BUT THE CANES PATTERNING THESE ARE UNIQUE. HELP IN MAKING SOMETHING SIMILAR WOULD HAVE TO COME FROM A SPECIALIST BOOK. HOWEVER, READY-MADE CANES WITH BEAUTIFUL DESIGNS ARE NOW INCREASINGLY AVAILABLE, AND A PROJECT LIKE THIS IS MORE ATTAINABLE. BY FOLLOWING THIS PROJECT YOU WILL ALSO BE INSPIRED TO HANG TOGETHER BEADS AND PENDANTS THAT YOU'VE MADE OR BOUGHT IN AN ENTIRELY NEW WAY.

YOU WILL NEED
Sharp blade
Metal or wood
    skewers
Baking tray
Oven with
    thermometer
Fuse wire needle
Hard cardboard
Scissors
Clear glue

FOR THE NECKLACE
The basic items listed
    below and the
    beads shown
    opposite:
Polymer clay
Silk thread
Ready-made canes
    (optional)

1 Prepare the polymer clay (see POLYMER CLAY) before starting to make your beads. Cut the beads to size, then pattern them with your own, or ready-made, canes. Shape the beads, pierce them and then bake them.

2 To make the pendant, model two colours of clay into two thick, square sheets. Pull the corners into an arc shape, and lay one square on top of the other, as shown. Decorate it with a yin-yang design (or one of your own) in different coloured clays, and decorate it with canes.

3 Make holes on the corners of the pendant where shown, and bake the piece flat on a baking tray.

4 Cut about 5m (4⅓yd) each of 14 silk threads to assemble the necklace. We have used seven different colours. Use a fuse wire needle to thread it through the beads.

5 Cut a one-third length of thread and put the first bead here. Leave plenty of spare thread and tie a knot. Add two more beads, knotting between them. Pass the thread through the top of the pendant.

6 Add three more beads in the same way on the other side, again leaving plenty of spare thread.

7 Cut another one-third length of thread. Leaving plenty of spare thread, add three beads. Make a larkshead knot from the back of the pendant through one corner hole. Add another knot, then thread back up the beads, knotting between them.

8 Knot the two cords together. Thread the final beads on this side, knotting between them.

26
CLAY CUBE BEADS

17
LARGE ROUND
CLAY BEADS

9 Repeat steps 7 and 8 for the other side.

10 Twist the cords above the knots after the last bead (see WORKING WITH THREADS).

11 Cut more silk to thread on the hanging beads. Work up from the bottom, leaving a length of thread, form a larkshead through the corner of the centrepiece, then knot back down to the bottom and make a tassel for the ends (see WORKING WITH THREADS).

INDONESIAN BIRD BEAD NECKLACE

THIS SIMPLE NECKLACE IS MADE WITH BEAUTIFUL HEAVY BEADS. THE SILVER BEADS AND THE ORNATE HOOK COME FROM BALI, WHERE WONDERFUL VARIETIES ARE HAND-CRAFTED; THE GLASS BEADS ARE COPIES OF THE TRADITIONAL "BIRD BEAD" DESIGNS. THESE BEADS ARE EXPENSIVE, SO THE BACK OF THE NECKLACE IS MADE FROM ORNATE KNOTTING THAT PICKS UP THE RED ON THE "BIRD BEAD" DESIGN.

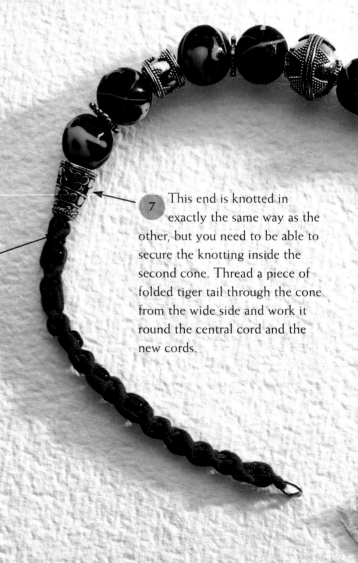

1 Cut a 50cm (20in) length of cord for threading. It will probably be too thick to use with a needle, so fold a small length of tiger tail in half and put the cord through it to help with the threading.

YOU WILL NEED
Scissors
Glue
Small piece of tiger tail for threading

FOR THE NECKLACE
The basic items listed below and the beads shown opposite:
2 silver cones
4 flat silver spacers
1 silver hook, with jump rings
2.5m (2⅔yd) red cord

8 As you knot on the new cords, pull the knots back into the cone while you are making them. When you have done the first four knots, and pulled them back into the cone, you can remove the piece of tiger tail from the cone. Knot and finish this side as before.

7 This end is knotted in exactly the same way as the other, but you need to be able to secure the knotting inside the second cone. Thread a piece of folded tiger tail through the cone from the wide side and work it round the central cord and the new cords.

3 Cut 1m (39in) of cord to do the knotting at this end. Push the beads back slightly and attach the central cord to the new cord, which should be double. Make four half knots (see WORKING WITH THREADS) and then pull them firmly into the cone to hide the join in the cords.

4 Make one more half knot and then put a 5mm glass bead on the central cord. Work the cords round this in the normal way so that the bead becomes part of the knotting. Make three more half knots and then add another bead. Continue in this way until you have worked five beads into the knotting on this side.

5 Decide on the length of your necklace and tie the central cord round the jump ring on the hook. Turn the rest of the central cord back towards the beads and continue to knot over both strands of the central cord.

2 Thread into one of the cones and work through the beads. Position the beads in the middle of the cord.

6 When you have knotted up to the hook pull the knotting cords as tightly as you can. Finish by using a needle or a piece of tiger tail to secure the ends of the cord back into the knotting. Put a drop of clear glue on the ends before you cut them.

10
GLASS "BIRD BEADS"

3
ROUND SILVER BEADS

2
TUBULAR SILVER BEADS

10
5MM BLACK GLASS BEADS

KNOTWORK PENDANT

KNOTTED NATURAL LINEN THREADS AND SUBTLY COLOURED EMBROIDERY COTTON MAKE THE PERFECT
BACKGROUND FOR DISPLAYING A FEW BEAUTIFUL, BEADS AND AN EXQUISITE
HAND-CARVED CHINESE PENDANT. YOU MAY NEED TO LEARN NEW TECHNIQUES, AND
THE WORK TAKES TIME, BUT THE RESULTS
ARE EXTREMELY REWARDING.

1 Make a full-size drawing of the necklace and pin it to your board so you can work over it, pinning on the work as you progress.

2 Cut six 3m (3¼yd) threads for each side and pull them through the pattern in the pendant so they are doubled. Tie one square knot (see WORKING WITH THREADS) using the outside cords to enclose all the threads.

3 Pin the two left-hand threads away from the others to use for knotting, then make clove hitches from left to right (see WORKING WITH THREADS).

4 Pin again at this side and using the same two threads make clove hitches from right to left (see WORKING WITH THREADS). Continue in snake-like curves, pinning at the corners, for about 5cm, (2in).

5 Take four cords on the left-hand side and make square knots for 5cm (2in), using two filler threads. Do the same on the right-hand side. In the middle work on the longer cylinder bead, making square knots at either side to keep the bead in place.

YOU WILL NEED
Soft pinboard
Pins
Scissors
Strong needle

FOR THE NECKLACE
The basic items listed below and the beads shown opposite:
36m (39yd) 5-ply linen thread, slightly waxed
Embroidery cotton in 3 colours
1 Chinese serpentine pendant
4 8mm glass beads
2 10mm Indonesian Pochuck nut beads (with large holes)
1 toggle bead

13 Repeat steps 2 and 3 on this side.

14 Using the first colour of your embroidery cottons, make two and a half rows of vertical clove hitches, letting the rest of the cotton hang down with the vertical thread.

15 Start your second colour on thread 7 and knot towards the right for a whole row, and to thread 8. As you work, knot over the hanging thread of the previous colour.

16 Begin the third colour where the second one finishes and knot for two more rows and six more threads in the vertical clove hitches, again enclosing your previous colours. Continue in this way as shown on the necklace.

17 Make another row of clove hitches, enclosing the ends of the embroidery cottons. Cut off the ends and make another row of clove hitches. Add two more glass beads as in step 6.

6 Using two left-hand threads as knotting threads repeat the clove hitches, working from left to right then right to left. Then thread the two glass beads on to the fourth and ninth threads from the left. Work two more rows of clove hitches.

7 Working with three groups of four threads, make six half knots.

11 Work all the threads through the toggle bead, positioning it 4cm (1½in) from the last bead. Pin the toggle down, then turn the board round, and make square knots back towards the last bead.

12 Cut off all the central threads, except the ones you are knotting with, close to the bead. Make a final square knot, then thread your knotting threads through the last bead, using a needle or wire, and clip the ends.

10 Divide the threads into two groups and make half knots for 4cm (1½in). Cut out two threads from the middle of each group as you work, then put one of the large Pochuk nut beads over the remaining threads.

9 Repeat step 4 for 2.5cm (1in).

8 Now leaving the two outside threads on each side, make square knots with threads 3 to 6 and 7 to 10, putting the flat bead on the central threads. Repeat the square knots and the half knots.

22 Start to make square knots 4cm (1½in) beyond the bead, and work them for 4.5cm (1¾in). Now turn the board round, and making a loop for the toggle, make square knots back towards your last bead, working over all the threads. Finish as you did on the first side.

21 Repeat step 10.

20 Repeat step 4.

18 Alternate rows of the square knots, using two knots together, for seven rows.

19 Make another row of clove hitches, from left to right, and put the cylinder bead on the four central threads, with an overhand knot above and below it (see WORKING WITH THREADS).

2
MATCHING
CYLINDER BEADS

1
ROUND POTTERY
GLAZED BEAD

THAI SILVER

CREATE A SENSATION WITH THIS DRAMATIC BELT MADE FROM HUNDREDS OF BEAUTIFUL SILVER BEADS. THE BEADS ARE MADE IN VILLAGES ON THE BORDERS OF THAILAND, USING TRADITIONAL SKILLS BROUGHT FROM CAMBODIA BY THE KHMER BEAD-MAKERS.

YOU WILL NEED
Necklace pliers
Large needles
Small needles
Scissors
Glue

FOR THE BELT
The basic items listed
 below and the
 beads shown
 opposite:
2 5mm (⅛in) jump
 rings
1 silver hook
12m (13yd) thick
 black polyester
 thread
2 medium patterned
 round beads
3 large patterned
 round beads
6 small patterned
 round beads
4 small patterned
 round beads
15 tiny tube beads
225 very tiny "sand"
 beads
4 small patterned
 round beads

FOR THE TASSELS
3 small "S" pieces
1.5m (5ft) thick black
 polyester thread
15 French crimps
30 4mm plain beads

1 Cut the thread in half and thread a strong but reasonably thin needle on to each piece. Put the needles in the centre of each thread so you are working with two double lengths. Knot the threads firmly together around one jump ring and put glue on the knot to secure it.

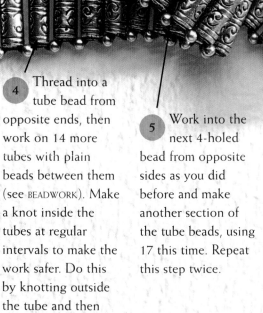

2 Position a small patterned bead over the knot when the glue is dry and pass both threads through the next two beads.

3 Separate the threads and work them through three plain small beads and one tiny patterned bead on either side. Thread both threads into the first large 4-holed bead and come out at the opposite corners. Add another tiny patterned bead and a plain bead to each thread.

4 Thread into a tube bead from opposite ends, then work on 14 more tubes with plain beads between them (see BEADWORK). Make a knot inside the tubes at regular intervals to make the work safer. Do this by knotting outside the tube and then pulling the knot inside it with the other thread.

5 Work into the next 4-holed bead from opposite sides as you did before and make another section of the tube beads, using 17 this time. Repeat this step twice.

* Reduce the number of tube beads and plain round beads to make a shorter belt – the one shown here is quite long.

6
LARGE 4-HOLED
BEADS

8 Knot the threads together and put glue onto the knot to secure it. When the glue is dry, cover the knot with a bead, add the others and put a single knot around the second jump ring. Work the threads back through the patterned beads but before pulling them tight put glue on the knot by the jump ring. When you pull the threads tight and pull the jump ring into the last patterned bead, the glue will hold the knot firm. Put the hook on the jump ring when the knot is secure.

7 Put on the last 4-holed bead section as before and follow with three more plain silver beads.

6 Work into the fifth 4-holed bead section and follow by weaving 20 tube beads.

192
4MM PLAIN
ROUND BEADS

24
TINY PATTERNED
ROUND BEADS

9 To make the tassels, cut five 10cm (4in) lengths of black thread and crimp them round a jump ring. Bring the threads through the patterned beads which will cover the crimps.

10 Work 15 of the tiny "sand" beads on to each thread adding a plain bead. Push all the beads back on their threads and then add some glue where the final plain bead will go. Thread on the bead, and when it is dry and secure cut the thread close to it.

86*
TUBE BEADS

CHINESE ENAMEL

THIS SET OF DELICATE JEWELLERY IS DESIGNED TO SHOW OFF THE CHARM OF THE ENAMELLED BEADS. CHINA HAS A LONG HISTORY OF BEAD-MAKING, AND NOWADAYS PRODUCES MANY FOR THE INTERNATIONAL MARKET. THE RAINBOW-COATED BEADS USED IN THIS SET COMPLEMENT THE ENAMELLED BEADS TO PERFECTION.

YOU WILL NEED
Round-nosed pliers
Wire cutters
2 needles
Glue

FOR THE CHOKER
The basic items listed
　below and the
　beads shown
　opposite:
74 3mm silver-plated
　balls
7 50mm (2in) eye
　pins
Fastener
120cm (4ft) thin
　polyester thread

FOR THE EARRINGS
10 3mm silver-plated
　balls
2 50mm (2in) eye
　pins
4 38mm (1½in) eye
　pins
2 ear wires
2 long enamelled
　beads
2 round enamelled
　beads
2 round enamelled
　beads with cut-out
　pattern

EARRINGS

1 To make the three earring sections use: a round bead with silver-plated balls on either side; a cut out bead with silver-plated balls on either side; and a long bead with a silver-plated ball above it.

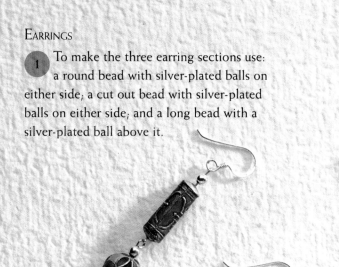

2 Open the loops at the tops of the eye pins to hang on the next section. Close them all neatly and add the ear wires.

5
ROUND
ENAMELLED BEADS

15
LONG ENAMELLED
BEADS

74
3MM SILVER-
PLATED BALLS

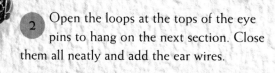

2 Cut two 60cm (24in) lengths of thread, and knot both together on to one side of your fastener (see FINISHING). There are four knots between the fastener and the first bead.

5 Repeat the pattern on the other side of the choker, making sure all the beads are neatly pushed together. Repeat the knotting on to the other side of the fastener.

3 Thread the silver-plated balls and rainbow coated beads on to both threads. Separate the threads. Put a silver-plated ball on each, then a long bead, and another silver-plated ball. Then join the threads together again to work through the next beads.

1 First make the hanging pieces in the same way as you would make straight earrings (see USING WIRE).

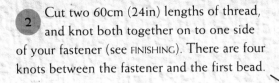

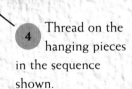

4 Thread on the hanging pieces in the sequence shown.

BROOCH
Make the hanging pieces for the brooch. Trim down the eye pins before you roll the tops to make loops, which you open sideways to hang the pieces.

24
RAINBOW-COATED
BEADS

2
ROUND CUT-OUT
PATTERNED
ENAMELLED BEADS

FOR THE BROOCH
1 ready-made brooch pin with loops
12 3mm silver-plated balls
4 50mm (2in) eye pins
2 long enamelled beads
1 round enamelled bead
1 round enamelled bead with cut-out pattern
2 5mm blue glass beads
4 rainbow-coated beads

BIRDS IN PARADISE

THE BEADS IN THIS NECKLACE COME FROM MANY DIFFERENT SOURCES, BUT THE RESULTING CREATION, WITH ITS LARGE PHILIPPINE FLOWERS AND BIRDS, AND VIVIDLY COLOURED FRUITS, EXUDES THE WARMTH OF THE SOUTH SEA ISLANDS. IF YOU PREPARE ALL THE PIECES IN ADVANCE THE NECKLACE IS EASY TO MAKE, AND IT WILL TURN MANY A HEAD.

YOU WILL NEED
Necklace pliers
Round-nosed pliers
Wire cutters

FOR THE NECKLACE
The basic items listed
  below and the
  beads shown
  opposite:
5 50mm (2in) head
  pins
17 38mm (1½in)
  head pins
2 50mm (2in) eye
  pins
Tiger tail
Fastener
French crimps
2 medium flowers
8 large lacquered
  beads
5 small lacquered
  beads
2 ornate plastic beads
2 cone beads
2 striped glass beads
87 wired glass drop
  beads
5 8mm round
  wooden beads
8 10mm black
  wooden beads
50 blue rocailles, size
  0/7
2 black rocailles, size
  0/8
5 blue tube beads

1 Wrap an eye pin round the neck of each bird, loop it through itself and thread on it three blue rocailles. Roll the top of the eye pin.

2 The fruits have wire stems. Thread each through a tube bead and a long bugle and roll the end of the wire.

9
LONG GLASS
BUGLES

1
VERY LARGE
FLOWER

2
EXOTIC BIRDS

7 Work round to the centre keeping a suitable number of pieces for the other side and thread into the birds and flowers.

8 Repeat on the other side, though your pattern need not be totally symmetrical. Thread the plainer beads again and finish with a cone to match the first side. Crimp into this side of the fastener.

6 Cut a length of tiger tail approximately 50cm (20in) long and crimp the fastener to one end. Allow a section of plainer beads, then build a glorious profusion of wired drops, fruits and beads. Thread the wired pieces as you would thread a bead.

5 Roll the wires on the little wired glass drop beads.

4 Thread five medium silk beads, six round lacquer beads and six 8mm wooden beads on 38mm (1½in) head pins with rocailles on either side of them. Roll the head pin for threading when you have clipped it to the required length.

3 Thread five of the small silk-covered beads on 50mm (2in) head pins, putting a rocaille at the bottom of each and a long bugle after each. Roll the tops of the head pins.

2
WOODEN WASHER
BEADS

6
MEDIUM SILK-
COVERED BEADS

13
SMALL SILK-
COVERED BEADS

5
ASSORTED FRUITS

SOO CHOW JADE

THIS REGAL CHOKER IS STRONGLY INFLUENCED BY THE EAST. THE BEADS ARE A MIXTURE OF SOO CHOW JADE AND FRESHWATER PEARLS, AND THE CENTREPIECE, WHICH IS REPEATED ON THE EARRINGS, IS MADE FROM CARVED SERPENTINE. THE RESULTING COMBINATION IS COOL AND ELEGANT.

YOU WILL NEED
Necklace pliers
Scissors
Needle
Round-nosed pliers

FOR THE NECKLACE
The basic items listed
    below and the
    beads shown
    opposite:
1 serpentine piece
4 metallized plastic
    spacer bars
2 bell caps
1 bolt ring
Short length of chain
2 25mm (1in) eye
    pins/0.8mm wire
8 French crimps
8m (8¾yd) thin white
    polyester thread

FOR THE EARRINGS
2 serpentine pieces
2 6mm Soo Chow
    jade beads
8 4mm Soo Chow
    jade beads
16 freshwater pearls
2 calottes
2 ear wires

1 Cut four 1m (39in) lengths of the thread and put two through each of the holes on one side of the serpentine piece. Thread a pearl, a 4mm jade bead and another pearl on each side of each of the threads.

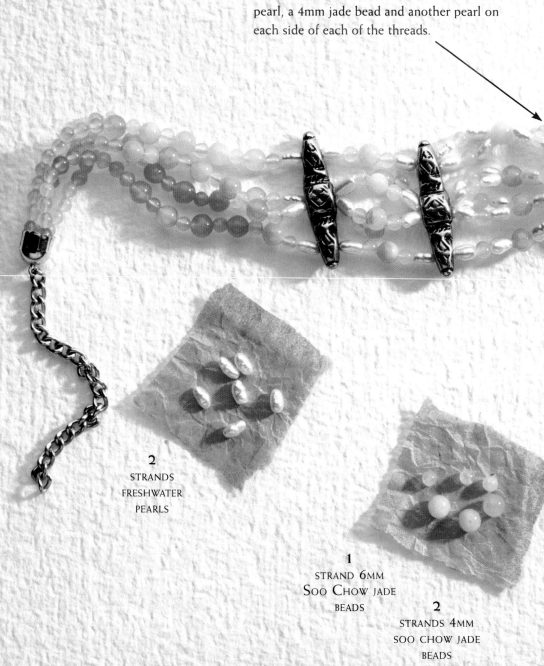

2
STRANDS
FRESHWATER
PEARLS

1
STRAND 6MM
SOO CHOW JADE
BEADS

2
STRANDS 4MM
SOO CHOW JADE
BEADS

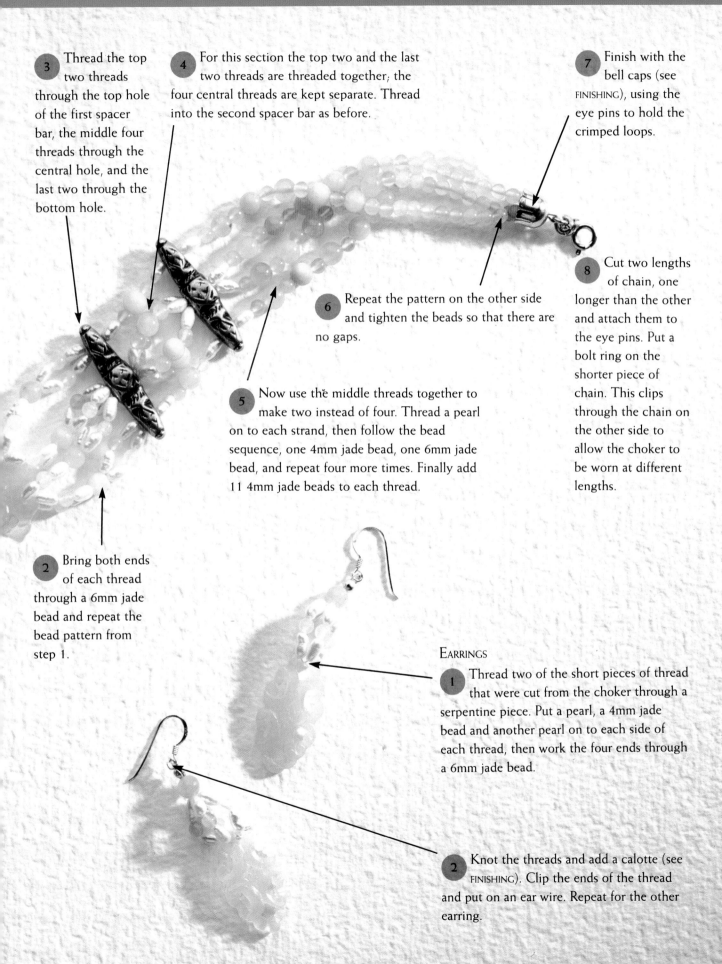

3 Thread the top two threads through the top hole of the first spacer bar, the middle four threads through the central hole, and the last two through the bottom hole.

4 For this section the top two and the last two threads are threaded together; the four central threads are kept separate. Thread into the second spacer bar as before.

7 Finish with the bell caps (see FINISHING), using the eye pins to hold the crimped loops.

6 Repeat the pattern on the other side and tighten the beads so that there are no gaps.

8 Cut two lengths of chain, one longer than the other and attach them to the eye pins. Put a bolt ring on the shorter piece of chain. This clips through the chain on the other side to allow the choker to be worn at different lengths.

5 Now use the middle threads together to make two instead of four. Thread a pearl on to each strand, then follow the bead sequence, one 4mm jade bead, one 6mm jade bead, and repeat four more times. Finally add 11 4mm jade beads to each thread.

2 Bring both ends of each thread through a 6mm jade bead and repeat the bead pattern from step 1.

EARRINGS

1 Thread two of the short pieces of thread that were cut from the choker through a serpentine piece. Put a pearl, a 4mm jade bead and another pearl on to each side of each thread, then work the four ends through a 6mm jade bead.

2 Knot the threads and add a calotte (see FINISHING). Clip the ends of the thread and put on an ear wire. Repeat for the other earring.

African beads

come in a variety of

materials and designs.

Since the earliest days of bone and shell, the continent

has developed the famous powder glass and dramatic Bodom

beads (Ghana), glass beads (from Bida in Nigeria), clay

beads (Morocco), Kiffa beads (Mauritania), dyed bone

(Kenya) meerschaum (Tanzania) and beautiful silver beads from Ethiopia.

At the height of the colonial trading period millions of pounds (weight) of European beads were exchanged for gold, palm oil and slaves. They were made in thousands of different designs and colours, ranging from the striking chevron beads to the tiny rocailles that are used for the beadwork that is so important in many African societies.

AFRICA

BEADS HAVE BEEN IMPORTANT WITHIN AFRICA FOR CENTURIES AS A FORM OF CURRENCY, A DISPLAY OF WEALTH AND AS SYMBOLS OF RELIGIOUS AND CULTURAL BELIEFS. OLD BEADS HAVE BEEN FOUND, AMONGST OTHER PLACES, IN BURIAL SITES, AROUND OLD WELLS WHERE TRADING HAS TAKEN PLACE, AND OFTEN IN LAKES AND RIVERS WHERE THEY HAVE BEEN PUT TO CALM THE WATERS.

BAOULE BRONZE

THE PENDANT PIECE ON THIS NECKLACE AND THE LOVELY GOLD COLOURED
BEADS ARE MADE USING LOST WAX CASTING BY THE BAOULE PEOPLE OF THE
IVORY COAST. THE GOLDEN BEADS ARE THREADED WITH TINY STRIPED AND
PLAIN VENETIAN BEADS AND SOME LARGE GHANAIAN BEADS
MADE FROM GROUND GLASS PUT INTO MOULDS AND REFIRED,
WITH THE COLOURS WORKED IN LAYERS AS THEY ARE FIRED.

3 Now divide the threads, taking three to each side of the necklace. Work each through three tiny beads and two flat beads, and then bring the three together again to pass through another flat bead and one powder glass bead.

YOU WILL NEED
Round-nosed pliers
Scissors
Needle
Glue

FOR THE NECKLACE
The basic items listed
  below and the
  beads shown
  opposite:
Bought hook and eye
  or wire to make
  one
2.25m (2½yd) thread
1 pendant

1 Cut three 75cm (2ft 6in) lengths of thread and put the pendant in the middle of them. Work all six threads through one of the flat Baoule beads.

2 Divide the threads and put each through three tiny beads and two flat beads, then work them back together through another flat bead.

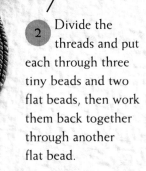

20
LONG BAOULE
BEADS

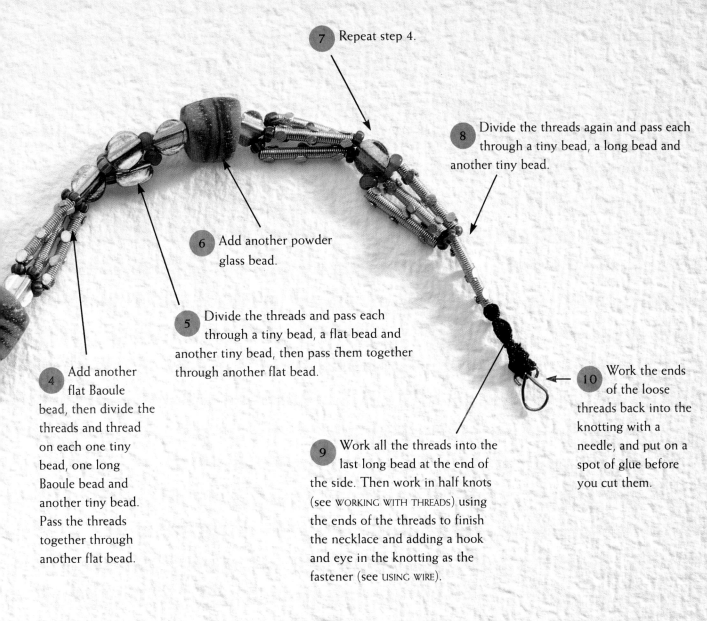

7 Repeat step 4.

8 Divide the threads again and pass each through a tiny bead, a long bead and another tiny bead.

6 Add another powder glass bead.

5 Divide the threads and pass each through a tiny bead, a flat bead and another tiny bead, then pass them together through another flat bead.

4 Add another flat Baoule bead, then divide the threads and thread on each one tiny bead, one long Baoule bead and another tiny bead. Pass the threads together through another flat bead.

9 Work all the threads into the last long bead at the end of the side. Then work in half knots (see WORKING WITH THREADS) using the ends of the threads to finish the necklace and adding a hook and eye in the knotting as the fastener (see USING WIRE).

10 Work the ends of the loose threads back into the knotting with a needle, and put on a spot of glue before you cut them.

42
FLAT BAOULE BEADS

4
POWDER GLASS BEADS

84
TINY VENETIAN BEADS, STRIPED AND PLAIN

AFRICAN COILS COLLAR

THIS COLLAR FEATURES TINY POWDER GLASS BEADS MADE IN GHANA FROM FINELY GROUND GLASS BOTTLES. THE BEAD-MAKERS FIRE THE BEADS IN MOULDS, CREATING COLOURFUL PATTERNS WITH DIFFERENT DYES. THE SMALL GLASS PENDANT SHAPES, MADE IN CZECHOSLOVAKIA FOR THE AFRICAN TRADE, ARE COPIES OF A "TALHAKIMT", A TRADITIONAL TUAREG DESIGN.

YOU WILL NEED
Round-nosed pliers
Needle
Adhesive tape

FOR THE NECKLACE
The basic items listed
   below and the
   beads shown
   opposite:
1.6m (63in) 0.8mm
   silver-plated wire
5m (5½yd) thick blue
   thread
4m (4⅓yd) thick
   yellow thread
18 25mm (1in) eye
   pins
9 Talhakimt shapes
   (6 blue, 3 yellow)
103 Blue faceted
   beads

1 Cut the wire into lengths to make the little coils (see USING WIRE).

2 With the pliers, open the loops at the bottom of the eye pins and hang on the coils. Thread beads on each eye pin, and roll the top. Make sure that your loop and the ready-made loop face in the same direction.

3 Cut a 3.5cm (1¼in) length of wire, roll a large loop at the bottom, and hang a blue talhakimt shape from it. Add beads as shown and roll a smaller loop at the top facing in the same direction as the bottom loop. Make another of these.

4 Cut a 4cm (1½in) length of wire and repeat step 3, adding another coil bead at the top before you roll. Repeat until you have two blue and two yellow talhakimt pieces, and one for the centre with the top loop at right angles to the bottom loop.

5 Cut two 1.5m (60in) lengths of blue thread and work them both through the first faceted bead. Push the bead about 30cm (12in) along the threads then start to weave the pattern (see BEADWORK).

6 After you have done this five times, put the first hanging piece on the bottom thread before you thread into a bead. Continue in this way, with the smaller coils on the outside, and the talhakimt pieces interspersed, until you reach the centre.

12 Repeat knotting and plaiting on the other side of the collar.

11 When you reach the talhakimt, undo the temporary knots, and using two long ends from the threads, bind them firmly around all the ends and knot them. Use a needle to work in these threads, then trim all the ends neatly.

8 Add 1m (39in) of yellow thread and make two half knots over your threads (see WORKING WITH THREADS). Put a temporary knot at the bottom.

10 Put your new piece of knotting around the knotting at the end of the collar, with the talhakimt at one side. Plait the three lengths together.

7 Now hang the central piece, which has the different loop. Work the pattern first, then open the loop and hang it round the threads that run through the central bead. Close the loop. Continue.

9 Cut 1m (39in) of the yellow thread and 1m (39in) of the blue thread and attach them in the middle to a talhakimt shape. Make another length of half knots working from the talhakimt.

50
MOROCCAN TILE
BEADS

25
POWDER GLASS
BEADS

12
COIL BEADS

OUT OF THE SOUK

THIS NECKLACE ECHOES BERBER JEWELLERY. MOST OF THE BEADS CAME FROM MOROCCO, AND IF YOU CAN'T MATCH THEM EXACTLY, JUST COPY THE FEELING OF THE PIECE — THE COLOURS AND SHAPES WILL STILL MAKE A PLEASING STATEMENT. IF YOU CAN'T OBTAIN A "HAND OF FATIMA", ANOTHER PENDANT PIECE, SUCH AS AN ENAMELLED BERBER ORNAMENT, WOULD WORK JUST AS WELL AS A CENTREPIECE.

2 Thread up on both sides of the necklace, using all three threads at once. Start with a tile bead, a coral glass bead and a tile bead.

1 Cut three 1m (39in) lengths of the thread and put them all through the centre of your pendant.

4 Repeat step 2. Then work the three strands together through a large Thai silver bead, a Moroccan clay bead, and another large Thai silver bead.

3 Work the three strands together through a large Moroccan clay bead. You may have to use a needle.

YOU WILL NEED
Necklace pliers
Scissors
Needle

FOR THE NECKLACE
The basic items listed below and the beads shown opposite:
1 "hand of Fatima"
2 silver cones
1 silver hook
2 silver rings
14 French crimps
3m (3¼yd) thick blue thread
4 Large Thai silver beads

146
SMALL
MOROCCAN TILE
BEADS

12
SMALL THAI
SILVER BEADS

5 Work on up the necklace, using the tile beads and coral glass beads between the other Thai silver beads and Moroccan clay beads.

6 Push the work back towards the centre of the necklace so that there are no gaps, then thread three more tile beads on to each strand at the ends of the necklace.

7 Attach the strands to each other with five of the crimps. Put a crimp on to two of the strands, then another crimp on two different strands, and so on. Push the crimps neatly towards the beads, and squeeze the crimps firmly with the pliers.

8 Clip off two of the loose threads and put the cone over the last thread, so that it covers all the crimping and loose ends.

9 Thread another crimp, a tile bead then another crimp after the cone. Work through the ring on the hook or the fastening ring, thread back through the crimps and the tile bead, and use a needle to work the thread back through the cone. Adjust the gaps around the crimps and the ring, and squeeze the crimps firmly.

10 Using sharp scissors, cut the loose ends on both sides.

96
CORAL GLASS
BEADS

8
ASSORTED
MOROCCAN CLAY
BEADS

AFRICAN FLOWERS

THE LITTLE FLOWERS AND VIBRANT COLOURS OF THIS DELICATE NECKLACE WERE INSPIRED BY ZULU
BEADWORK. IT IS NOT A PROJECT TO CONTEMPLATE IN A RUSH, BUT THE TECHNIQUES ARE NOT DIFFICULT
IF APPROACHED WITH PATIENCE AND DEXTERITY. THE REWARDS OF SEEING THE NECKLACE BUILD SECTION
BY SECTION ARE WELL WORTH THE EFFORT.

1 Start by weaving rows of 8 rocailles which stand side by side to make a band (see BEADWORK). Continue in this way until you have 165 rows. When you have finished the rows take your thread back through all of them to strengthen the work and keep an even tension.

11 Bring a new thread up through the middle of the last row of work. Thread on approximately seven black rocailles and then a Venetian bead. Repeat until you have three Venetian beads, then add three more black rocailles and work back through all the beads and rocailles. Re-work this several times for security, then finish by taking the thread back through the main necklace to secure it.

YOU WILL NEED
Plenty of beading
    needles
Very sharp scissors
Glue/nail varnish to
    finish ends of
    thread
Beeswax (optional)

FOR THE NECKLACE
The basic items listed
    below and the
    beads shown
    opposite:
10m (12yd) black
    polycotton thread

2 Build more rocailles above these rows (see BEADWORK). Repeat this technique along the top of the necklace.

4 Sew in a new thread at a po[...] rocailles from the middle. [...] same technique as in step 2, be[...] row following the colours show[...] again, using the appropriate colour[...] colour changes in the 3rd row you hav[...] complete row of flowers.

3 Do the same as you have done on the top row in step 2, but add two rows of black rocailles to this side.

Note: rubbing beeswax on the thread strengthens it and makes it less likely to tangle.

10 Make the buttonhole loop by threading approximately 19 rocailles (depending on the size of your Venetian beads). Sew securely back through the loop and the necklace several times.

9 Add a new thread, and start with the needle through the last rocaille in the row. Add three coloured rocailles before threading back into it. Then take the needle down through the next rocaille in the row and add three more coloured rocailles. Repeat this all round the edges except where the fringes hang.

8 This fringe is made in the same way as in step 7 but the strands have alternately 8 and 10 black rocailles.

7 To make the fringes (see BEADWORK) add a new thread and work with 16 and 14 black rocailles alternating with three coloured rocailles at the bottom. Repeat on the other side of the necklace.

6 Counting towards the middle, start another row of flowers between the eleventh and twelfth rocailles. You will add 24 rocailles and start to make six more flowers. Work on as before until you have made two more rows of flowers and finish the work with a black row.

5 Make one row of black rocailles, then begin another row of flowers on the next row and work as before. Repeat until you have three rows of flowers, with a black row between each and as the last row.

18g (¾oz) ROCAILLES OF EACH OF: RED, YELLOW, BLUE, TURQUOISE, ORANGE, DARK GREEN, LIGHT GREEN, SIZE 0/11

100g (4oz) BLACK ROCAILLES SIZE 0/11

3 8MM VENETIAN MILLEFIORE BEADS

KAZURI CERAMICS

KAZURI, WHICH MEANS "SMALL AND BEAUTIFUL" IN SWAHILI, IS THE NAME OF A COMPANY SET UP

17 YEARS AGO IN NAIROBI, KENYA, TO EMPLOY LOCAL WOMEN TO MAKE CERAMIC BEADS BY HAND.

THESE THREE HEAVY AND DRAMATIC NECKLACES, AND THE BEADS

FROM WHICH THEY WERE MADE, WERE DESIGNED BY KAZURI.

YOU WILL NEED
Necklace pliers

FOR THE NECKLACE
The basic items listed
   below and the
   beads shown
   opposite:
Tiger tail
French crimps
Fasteners
Large round plain
   brass beads
Small round plain
   brass beads
Tiny metal spacer
   beads
Black rocailles, size
   0/8
Fluted elliptical brass
   beads

1 These necklaces are made in varying lengths, 80cm (31in), 87cm (34in) and 68cm (27in).

2 Cut a length of tiger tail to the length required and thread the central bead on it.

3 These necklaces are all symmetrical, with black rocailles and brass washers between the bigger beads. Arrange your beads using the ideas shown, or to your own design.

4 Crimp the ends of the thread on to the fasteners. (see FINISHING.)

Note: If you are unable to get such a wide selection of beads as we have shown here, you could pattern plain beads with cold ceramic paints or varnishes. You could even make your own beads at a ceramics class!

ASSORTED KAZURI BEADS

AFRICAN POWERS

THIS STARK, STRONG NECKLACE IS DESIGNED TO ECHO THE ORIGINS OF THE BEADS. THE BIG BONE BEADS COME FROM KENYA; THE SMALL STRIPED ONES ARE SOME OF THE THOUSANDS OF TONS OF BEADS MADE IN VENICE IN THE LAST CENTURY WHICH WERE SENT IN TRADING SHIPS DOWN THE COASTS OF AFRICA.

YOU WILL NEED
Needle
Glue

FOR THE NECKLACE
The basic items listed
    below and the
    beads shown
    opposite:
8 coil beads
6m (5½yd) thick
    black thread
10 Wide matt black
    glass beads
1 Horn bead for
    fastener

2 Work around the necklace joining and separating the threads into the different beads as shown, near the end pass all the strands through another wide glass bead and add more rocailles on each thread.

1 Cut four 1m (39in) lengths of thread and pass them all through the central bone bead. Working on one side, thread two rocailles, a striped bead, and two more rocailles on each thread and then work them all back together into another bone bead, followed by a wide glass bead.

272
BLACK ROCAILLES,
SIZE 0/7

5 Make this plaiting into a loop for your buttonhole. Face all the central threads back towards the beads, and continue to knot with the other threads, so the loose threads are neatly worked inside. Finish knotting when the buttonhole is the correct size for the horn bead.

4 Using half knots, work the new threads over the existing ones (see WORKING WITH THREADS). About 4cm (1½in) away from your final length, stop knotting and plait the central strands together.

3 Cut another 1m (39in) length of thread, fold it in half to use double and attach it firmly to the strands you have been working with. Pass the resulting eight threads through a final wide glass bead on this side.

8 Finally, using a needle, work the ends of the threads back into the knotting, put a tiny drop of glue on each strand, and cut them very close to the work.

7 Attach knotting threads in the same way on this side, and repeat the half knots. When you are 4cm (1½in) from the finished length thread two of the central threads through the horn bead and turn their ends back towards the centre of the necklace. Trim the other central threads close to the button bead and finish the knotting, working up to the button bead.

6 Work this side of the necklace in the same way, and push all the beads firmly towards the end you have knotted to ensure there are no gaps.

96
STRIPED
VENETIAN beads

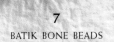

7
BATIK BONE BEADS

MAURITANIAN MYSTERIES

THIS NECKLACE USES LOVELY OLD SILVER BEADS AND A VERY COLLECTABLE KIFFA BEAD FROM MAURITANIA. THE OLD SILVER BEADS AND EXQUISITE SILVER SHAPES ARE WORKED TOGETHER WITH OLD STRIPED VENETIAN BEADS, "WHITE HEARTS," AND SOME MODERN GLASS BEADS. THE THREADING IS SIMPLE, BUT THE ENDS ARE KNOTTED TO GIVE EXTRA EMPHASIS TO THE SPECIAL BEADS.

1 Cut four 1m (39in) lengths of thread and arrange them on your work-surface, leaving space between them. Start to position the beads. In a design like this, the arrangement can be fairly random, but remember not to position large beads too close together, and to space all your colours and shapes evenly.

2 The Kiffa bead goes in the centre of the longest thread. Save two of the Venetian striped beads to go at the ends, and one large silver bead as a fastener.

YOU WILL NEED
Scissors
Needle
Glue

FOR THE NECKLACE
The basic items listed
  below and the
  beads shown
  opposite:
2 large silver shapes
37 small silver shapes
8.5m (9⅓yd) thick
  black polyester
  thread
1 Kiffa bead
2 Large silver
  Mauritanian beads
57 Tiny silver beads
9 Larger silver beads
4 Glazed blue tile
  beads

2
SILVER MALI
BEADS

53
5MM BLACK
GLASS BEADS

12
FACETED BLUE
GLASS BEADS

4 Cut a 4m (4⅓yd) length of thread for each side for the knotting. Using these threads double, tie them tightly round the beaded threads close to the last small beads. Carefully work all eight strands of thread through a striped bead, then make half knots (see WORKING WITH THREADS) until both sides of the necklace are approximately 4cm (1½in) shorter than your intended necklace length.

5 Thread the central threads through the fastening bead and fold the ends back. Continue knotting half knots over these threads to secure them. Finish knotting under the fastening bead.

3 Hold the beads up in front of you to make sure that the strands hang well together.

6 For the other side of your work, add 50cm (19½in) of thread and make a small section of buttonholing (see WORKING WITH THREADS). Match the length of your ends and turn the loose ends on this side back towards the centre using the knotting to cover them. Work over a little of the buttonholing until you have created the right size loop for your fastening bead.

7 Work the ends of the threads back into the knotting with a needle and use a drop of glue before you trim them.

22
SMALL RED STRIPED
VENETIAN BEADS

238
BLACK ROCAILLES, SIZE 0/7

9
LARGER RED STRIPED
VENETIAN BEADS

14
DARK RED ROCAILLES, SIZE 0/7

27
RED "WHITE HEARTS"

13
ASSORTED BLUE STRIPED
VENETIAN BEADS

WEDDING BEADS

BOTH OF THE MAIN TYPES OF BEADS IN THIS DESIGN ARE MADE IN THE FORMER CZECHOSLOVAKIA, ORIGINALLY FOR THE AFRICAN MARKET. THE TEARDROP-SHAPED BEADS, ASSOCIATED WITH MARRIAGE, ARE COMMONLY KNOWN AS WEDDING BEADS; THE TRIANGULAR BEADS WERE MADE TO REPLACE THE VALUED CONUS SHELL BEADS FORMERLY USED AS CURRENCY IN EAST AFRICA, WHICH WERE DESTROYED BY THE BRITISH, WHO CONSIDERED THEM PAGAN.

YOU WILL NEED
Necklace pliers
Scalpel
Scissors
Round-nosed pliers

FOR THE NECKLACE
The basic items listed
   below and the
   beads shown
   opposite:
2 leather or lace end
   crimps
hook and ring/0.8mm
   wire
150cm (60in) tiger
   tail
6 French crimps
1 large triangle
2 red rocailles,
   size 0/7

FOR THE EARRINGS
18cm 0.8mm silver-
   plated wire
8cm (3in) black
   plastic tubing
2 ear wires
10 wedding beads

EARRINGS
Cut two 8cm (3in) lengths of the silver-plated wire and form them into hoops (see WIRING), leaving one end unturned. Cut four 2cm (¾in) lengths of the tubing and thread the beads and tubing on to the hoop. Turn the other side of the hoop, add the jump ring and hook on the ear wire. Repeat for the other earring.

7 Repeat the pattern of beads on this side of the necklace.

70
BLUE ROCAILLES,
SIZE 0/7

15
SMALL TRIANGLES

10 Fix the leather crimp to this end and attach a hook to it. Cut the ends of the tiger tail with a scalpel so none is left showing above the leather crimp.

6 Use French crimps so the strands are all held together.

9 Gently wrap both sides of the leather crimp round the French crimps so they are covered, and then squeeze firmly. Attach the ring to the leather crimp.

5 Work all three strands through four wedding beads with rocailles between them, and on into six small triangles with rocailles between them. Finish with three rocailles.

8 Push all the beads towards the finished side and make sure there are no gaps in the work, before finishing.

4 Now work two of the strands together into another five wedding beads with rocailles between them. Use the other strand singly with the same arrangement. Repeat step 3.

3 Work the three strands into a rocaille, a small triangle and another rocaille.

2 Separate the strands and thread five wedding beads on to each, with a rocaille between each bead.

1 Cut three 50cm (20in) lengths of tiger tail and thread the large triangle into the middle of them, followed by one of the blue rocailles.

58
WEDDING BEADS

TREASURES FROM AFRICA

THE CROSS IS MADE BY SILVERSMITHS IN ETHIOPIA, BUT THE PATTERNED GLASS BEADS, OFTEN CALLED AFRICAN TRADING BEADS, WERE MADE IN VENICE AND SHIPPED DOWN THE AFRICAN COASTS UNTIL THE 1930S. THEY ARE CALLED MILLEFIORE BEADS, AND WERE MADE IN THOUSANDS OF DIFFERENT DESIGNS. IN 1880 EXPERTS SAY THE VENETIANS MADE AS MUCH AS 2,720,000KG (6,000,000LB) OF GLASS BEADS, A LARGE PROPORTION OF WHICH WOULD HAVE BEEN OF THIS TYPE. THE CZECHOSLOVAKIANS ALSO MADE VAST AMOUNTS OF BEADS FOR THE AFRICAN TRADE, AND THE PLAIN GLASS BEADS IN THIS NECKLACE WERE PROBABLY MADE THERE AND TRADED TO NIGERIA. NOWADAYS MANY OF THE BEADS THAT WERE ORIGINALLY SENT FROM EUROPE TO AFRICA HAVE BEEN TRADED BACK INTO EUROPE AND THE UNITED STATES, SO YOU SHOULD BE ABLE TO FIND A SUPPLIER QUITE EASILY.

YOU WILL NEED
Necklace pliers
Round-nosed pliers
File (if needed to
    make hook)

FOR THE NECKLACE
The basic items listed
    below and the
    beads shown
    opposite:
Ethiopian cross
75cm (30in) leather
    thonging
2 spring ends
Hook, or 8mm
    (⅜in) wire to make
    a hook

FOR THE BRACELET
18cm (7in) approx.
    leather thonging
2 spring ends
1 spring clasp
1 small Venetian
    glass bead
10 Czech glass beads
12 plain black bone
    beads

FOR THE EARRINGS
2 50mm (2in) eye
    pins
2 ear wires
2 small Venetian
    glass beads
2 Czech glass beads
4 plain bone beads
6 3mm silver-plated
    balls

1 Cut your thonging to the required length.

BRACELET
The bracelet is made in the same way as the necklace, but the top loops on the spring ends are opened sideways to attach the clasp. Don't forget to check the length you require before you start.

EARRINGS
Put beads onto eye pins. Roll the tops of the eye pins and add the ear wires.

3 To attach the spring ends, put each one over either end of the leather thong and press the last coil of the spring into the leather. Make sure it is firmly held.

4 Attach the hook to one of the spring ends by opening the loop on the hook sideways with the round-nosed pliers, slipping it through the loop on the end of the spring, then closing it again with the pliers.

2 Thread the beads on the leather in the pattern shown, or to suit your own combination of beads.

44
PLAIN BLACK BONE
BEADS

14
VENETIAN GLASS
BEADS

28
CZECH GLASS
BEADS

2
OLD SILVER BEADS

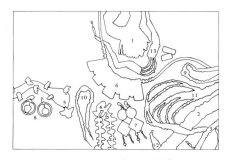

AMERICA   (pages 26-7)
1, 2 and 3 from The Trading Post
4 and 5 from Neal Street East
6, 7, 8, 9 and 10 from Pachacuti
11, 12 and 13 from Tumi

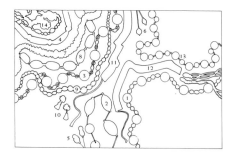

EUROPE   (pages 48-9)
1, 2, 3 and 4 from Joka
5 and 6 from J T Morgan
7, 8, 9, 10, 11, 12, 13 and
14 privately owned

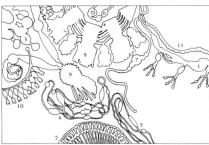

MIDDLE EAST   (pages 68-9)
1 and 2 from Egyptian Bazaar
3, 4 and 5 from Ethnic World
6 and 7 from Necklace Maker Workshop
8 lent by Sheila Paine
9 Amaz Ltd
10 privately owned
11 Berber Design

FAR EAST   (pages 88-9)
1, 2, 3, 4, 5, 6, 7, 8 and 9 from the
collection of Carole Morris
10 and 11 from Neal Street East
12 from Necklace Maker Workshop
13 and 14 privately owned

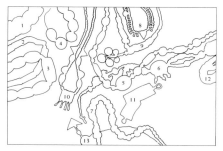

AFRICA   (pages 108-9)
1, 2, 3 and 4 from African Accents
5 and 6 from Berber Design
7 from Neal Street East
8 privately owned
9, 10, 11, 12 and 13 Oxfam Trading

PROJECT DESIGNERS

The author designed all the projects except those listed below. Contact Sara Withers at: Bojangles, Old Cottage, Appleton, Abingdon, OXON OX13 5JH England. Commissions accepted.

Crow Indian Bracelet; Bamboo Bird's Wing: Denise Weiss, 17 The Carltons, Elgin Mews North, London W9 1NN England. Commissions.

African Flowers: Evelyn Cohen, Oxbrook Cottage, Coombs, Near Lancing, West Sussex, BW15 0RS England. Commissions for beadwork accepted.

Kazuri Ceramics: Kazuri Ltd, PO Box 24276 Nairobi, Kenya. Bead suppliers.

Phoenix Rising: Akiko Kase, 185A Portobello Road, London W11 2ED England. Commissions accepted.

Edwardian Choker: Elise Mann, The Crafty Owl, 54 Tiverton Road, Edgware, Middx HA8 6BC England. Commissions accepted.

Braided Cord Pendant: Rodrick Owen, Lakeside House, 41 Lake Street, Oxford OX1 4RW England. Commissions accepted. The large bead was from Bedazzled, Baltimore, USA. It was created by Nancy Potek. Silk thread: Kumihimo silk from Japan.

Knotwork Pendant: Jane Olson, 919 Bromley Drive, Baton Rouge, LA 70808 USA. Commissions accepted.

Thai Silver; Eastern Influence: Tito and Jane Haggardt, PO Box 7099, Ocean View, Hawaii 96737 USA. Bead suppliers.

Colourful Polymer: Ann Baxter, The Cromlech, Cromlech Road, Ardnadam, By Dunoon, Argyll, Scotland PA23 8QH. Bead supplier.

Birds in Paradise; Indian Silver and Amethyst: Erica Steinhauer, 40 Cowley Road, Oxford OX4 1HZ England.

Pre-Columbian Inspirations: Juana Gelen, The Peruvian Bead Company, 1601 Callens Road, Ventura, CA 93003 USA. Bead suppliers.

Bohemian Chains: Catherine Popesco, Au Bout des Rêves, Zone Artisanale Le Cluzel, 42600 Lezigneux France. Bead supplier.

Crowning Jewels: Hobby Horse Ltd, 15-17 Langton Street, London SW10 0JL England. Bead suppliers.

Lindisfarne Twist: Carole Morris. The beads for this design are obtainable from: Spangles, 1 Casburn Lane, Burwell, Cambridge, England CB5 0ED. Send SAE for current catalogue.

Ancient and Modern: Janet Coles Beads Ltd, Perdiswell Cottage, Bilford Road, Worcester WR3 8QA England. Bead suppliers.

Native American Inspirations: Schmuck-art, Peter Hegewisch Gmbh, Rudi-Ismayr-Str. 1a, 85375 Neufahrn, Germany. Bead suppliers.

Other beads supplied by:

Ahenzi Beads, Flema, Chilton Foliat, Hungerford, England. Balagan, Eye, Cambridgeshire, England. Beaded Toucan, Friday Harbour, WA, USA. Beadworks, London, England and Norwalk CT,

USA. Creative Beadcraft Ltd, Amersham, Bucks, England. Freedom Touch, Soquel, CA, USA. Picard, Carmel, CA, USA.

The Trading Post, Arts/Crafts Centre, 40 Middle Yard, Camden Lock, London NW1 8AF England.

Neal Street East, 5 Neal Street, Covent Garden, London WC2H 9PU England.

Pachacuti, Old Stone Lodge, Musbury Road, Axmouth, Seaton, EX12 4BP England.

Tumi, 23 Chalk Farm Road, London, NW1 8AG England.

Joka (masks, jewellery and Venetian glass), 48 West Yard, Camden Lock Place, London NW1 8AF England.

J T Morgan (Haberdashery), 28 Chepstow Cnr, Chepstow Place, London W2 4XA England.

Egyptian Bazaar at Museum Gallery, 19 Bury Place, London WC1 2JH England.

Ethnic World, 71 Berwick Street, London W1V 3PE England.

Necklace Maker Workshop, 259 Portobello Road, London W11 1LR England.

Amaz Ltd, 16 Crescent West, Hadley Wood, Hertfordshire, England.

African Accents, 23 Ostade Road, London SW2 2AZ England.

Berber Design, 84 Highgate High Street, London N6 5HX England.

Oxfam Trading, Murdock Road, Bicester, Oxon OX6 7RF.